THE OVERWROUGHT URN

The Overwrought Urn

>>>>>>>>>>>>>>>>>>

*a potpourri of parodies
of critics who triumphantly
present the real meaning
of authors from
Jane Austen to J. D. Salinger*

Edited by
Charles Kaplan

PEGASUS  NEW YORK

Library of Congress Catalog Card Number 69-15221

ACKNOWLEDGMENTS

"Pierre Menard, Author of Don Quixote." Translated by Anthony Bonner. From FICCIONES by Jorge Luis Borges. Reprinted by permission of Grove Press, Inc. Copyright © 1962 by Grove Press, Inc. Also reprinted by permission of Weidenfeld and Nicolson, Ltd., London. "The Warp and the Wolf." From FROM BEOWULF TO VIRGINIA WOOLF, copyright © 1952 by Robert Manson Myers. Reprinted by permission of the publishers, The Bobbs-Merrill Company, Inc. "The Transcendentalists" From AMERICAN LIT RELIT by Richard Armour. Copyright © 1964 by Richard Armour. Used by permission of McGraw-Hill Book Company. "Thomas Mann and Eighteenth-Century Comic Fiction." From *Furioso,* Winter, 1951. Copyright © 1951 by Reed Whittemore. Reprinted by permission of Reed Whittemore and the author, Wayne Booth. "How to Criticize A Poem." Reprinted by Permission of *The New Republic,* © 1943, Harrison-Blaine of New Jersey, Inc. "The Greatest English Lyric?—A New Reading of Joe E. Skilmer's 'Therese'" Reprinted by permission of the author, John Frederick Nims, and by permission of the Bibliographical Society of the University of Virginia. "Eliot Among the Nightingales: Fair and Foul." Copyright © 1954, by The University of New Mexico. Reprinted from the *New Mexico Quarterly,* Summer, 1954. "Invictus: A Regurgitation." Reprinted from HOPA-LONG FREUD by Ira Wallach. By permission of Abelard-Schuman, Ltd. All rights reserved. Copyright year 1951. "The Ghost of Christmas Past: 'Stopping by Woods on A Snowy Evening.'" Reprinted from *College English,* December, 1962, with the permission of the National Council of Teachers of English and Herbert R. Coursen, Jr. "The Secret of the Secret Sharer Bared." Reprinted from *College English,* October, 1965, with the permission of the National Council of Teachers of English and Bruce Harkness. "Mrs. Bennet and the Dark Gods." From *The Sewanee Review;* October, 1956. Copyright © 1956 by the University of the South. Reprinted in ENGAGED AND DISENGAGED, by Douglas Bush, Harvard University Press, 1966. Reprinted by permission of the author, *The Sewanee Review,* and Harvard University Press. "Eloise Disclosed." Reprinted from SCRAP IRONY by Felicia Lamport, with the permission of the publishers, Houghton Mifflin Company. Copyright © 1961 by Felicia Lamport. Also reprinted with the permission of Victor Gollancz Ltd., London. "Patristic Exegesis: *Tom Sawyer.*" Reprinted from *College English,* October, 1965, with the

The present study grew out of a doctoral disputation written at a well-known continental finishing school; it appears now only after years of expensive revision and diligent research at the Harvard Theological Cemetery and the British Mausoleum. Grateful acknowledgment is hereby extended to my wife, who has requested that I withhold her name from the Index.

Foreword

"To hell with criticism; praise is good enough for me."
—*Tallulah Bankhead*

"The borer on our peach trees bores that she may deposit an egg; but the borer into books bores that he may bore."
—*Ralph Waldo Emerson*

~ It is a truism to say that this is an Age of Criticism. Never have so many journals of criticism flourished, never have so many graduate students been busy writing critical dissertations, never have so many professors of literature ground out notes, articles, and books attempting to cast light on the received literary canon. And never has there been so much nonsense written in the name of criticism. In our eagerness to explicate the most super-subtle shadings of meaning, or to apply the insights of depth psychology, anthropology, or mythology, we have committed excesses of shuddering inanity. To parody excess is an almost impossible task; as several of the writers in this collection have discovered to their dismay, what was written as parody was taken seriously by some readers.

But all writing about literature is guilty of special forms of nonsense: the time-bound historians, the literary gossips, the humorless researchers are equally targets for the parodist. In the hope that parody, itself a form of criticism, can provide a salutary gust of fresh air, this collection has been assembled to blow a few academic minds. It is no accident that most of the authors in this collection are themselves critics and teachers of literature; it is a hopeful sign when the professional literati can laugh at themselves.

C.K.

Northridge, California

Contents

THE OVERWROUGHT URN

The Historical View
>>>>>>>>>>>>>>>>>>>>>>>>>>>>>>>>

Pierre Menard, Author of Don Quixote

⟳ The *visible* works left by this novelist are easily and briefly enumerated. It is therefore impossible to forgive the omissions and additions perpetrated by Madame Henri Bachelier in a fallacious catalogue that a certain newspaper, whose Protestant tendencies are no secret, was inconsiderate enough to inflict on its wretched readers—even though they are few and Calvinist, if not Masonic and circumcised. Menard's true friends regarded this catalogue with alarm, and even with a certain sadness. It is as if yesterday we were gathered together before the final marble and the fateful cypresses, and already Error is trying to tarnish his Memory. . . . Decidedly, a brief rectification is inevitable.

I am certain that it would be very easy to challenge my meager authority. I hope, nevertheless, that I will not be prevented from mentioning two important testimonials. The Baroness de Bacourt (at whose unforgettable *vendredis* I had the honor of becoming acquainted with the late lamented poet) has seen fit to approve these lines. The Countess de Bagnoregio, one of the most refined minds in the Principality of Monaco (and now of Pittsburgh, Pennsylvania, since her recent marriage to the international philanthropist Simon Kautsch who, alas, has been so slandered by the victims of his disinterested handiwork) has sacrificed to "truth and death" (those are her words) that majestic reserve which distinguishes her, and in an open letter published in the magazine *Luxe* also grants me her consent. These authorizations, I believe, are not insufficient.

I have said that Menard's *visible* lifework is easily enumerated. Having carefully examined his private archives, I have been able to verify that it consists of the following:

a) A symbolist sonnet which appeared twice (with variations) in the magazine *La Conque* (the March and October issues of 1899).

b) A monograph on the possibility of constructing a poetic vocabulary of concepts that would not be synonyms or periphrases of those which make up ordinary language, "but ideal objects created by means of common agreement and destined essentially to fill poetic needs" (Nîmes, 1901).

c) A monograph on "certain connections or affinities" among the ideas of Descartes, Leibnitz and John Wilkins (Nîmes, 1903).

d) A monograph on the *Characteristica Universalis* of Leibnitz (Nîmes, 1904).

e) A technical article on the possibility of enriching the game of chess by means of eliminating one of the rooks' pawns. Menard proposes, recommends, disputes, and ends by rejecting this innovation.

f) A monograph on the *Ars Magna Generalis* of Ramón Lull (Nîmes, 1906).

g) A translation with prologue and notes of the *Libro de la invención y arte del juego del axedrez* by Ruy López de Segura (Paris, 1907).

h) The rough draft of a monograph on the symbolic logic of George Boole.

i) An examination of the metric laws essential to French prose, illustrated with examples from Saint-Simon (*Revue des langues romanes,* Montpellier, October, 1909).

j) An answer to Luc Durtain (who had denied the existence of such laws) illustrated with examples from Luc Durtain (*Revue des langues romanes,* Montpellier, December, 1909).

k) A manuscript translation of the *Aguja de navegar cultos* of Quevedo, entitled *La boussole des précieux.*

l) A preface to the catalogue of the exposition of lithographs by Carolus Hourcade (Nîmes, 1914).

m) His work, *Les problèmes d'un problème* (Paris, 1917), which takes up in chronological order the various solutions of the famous problem of Achilles and the tortoise. Two editions of this book have appeared so far; the second has as an epigraph Leibnitz' advice "Ne craignez point, monsieur, la tortue," and contains revisions of the chapters dedicated to Russell and Descartes.

n) An obstinate analysis of the "syntactic habits" of Toulet (*N.R.F.*, March, 1921). I remember that Menard used to declare that censuring and praising were sentimental operations which had nothing to do with criticism.

o) A transposition into Alexandrines of *Le Cimetière marin* of Paul Valéry (*N.R.F.*, January, 1928).

p) An invective against Paul Valéry in the *Journal for the Suppression of Reality* of Jacques Reboul. (This invective, it should be stated parenthetically, is the exact reverse of his true opinion of Valéry. The latter understood it as such, and the old friendship between the two was never endangered.)

q) A "definition" of the Countess of Bagnoregio in the "victorious volume"—the phrase is that of another collaborator, Gabriele d'Annunzio—which this lady publishes yearly to rectify the inevitable falsifications of journalism and to present "to the world and to Italy" an authentic effigy of her person, which is so exposed (by reason of her beauty and her activities) to erroneous or hasty interpretations.

r) A cycle of admirable sonnets for the Baroness de Bacourt (1934).

s) A manuscript list of verses which owe their effectiveness to punctuation.*

Up to this point (with no other omission than that of

---

*Madame Henri Bachelier also lists a literal translation of a literal translation done by Quevedo of the *Introduction à la vie dévote* of Saint Francis of Sales. In Pierre Menard's library there are no traces of such a work. She must have misunderstood a remark of his which he had intended as a joke.

some vague, circumstantial sonnets for the hospitable, or
greedy, album of Madame Henri Bachelier) we have the
visible part of Menard's works in chronological order. Now
I will pass over to that other part, which is subterranean,
interminably heroic, and unequaled, and which is also—oh,
the possibilities inherent in the man!—inconclusive. This
work, possibly the most significant of our time, consists of
the ninth and thirty-eighth chapters of Part One of *Don
Quixote* and a fragment of the twenty-second chapter. I
realize that such an affirmation seems absurd; but the
justification of this "absurdity" is the primary object of this
note.*

Two texts of unequal value inspired the undertaking. One
was that philological fragment of Novalis—No. 2005 of the
Dresden edition—which outlines the theme of *total* identification with a specific author. The other was one of those
parasitic books which places Christ on a boulevard, Hamlet
on the Cannebière and Don Quixote on Wall Street. Like
any man of good taste, Menard detested these useless
carnivals, only suitable—he used to say—for evoking plebeian
delight in anachronism, or (what is worse) charming us
with the primary idea that all epochs are the same, or that
they are different. He considered more interesting, even
though it had been carried out in a contradictory and
superficial way, Daudet's famous plan: to unite in *one*
figure, Tartarin, the Ingenious Gentleman and his squire. . . .
Any insinuation that Menard dedicated his life to the writing of a contemporary *Don Quixote* is a calumny of his
illustrious memory.

He did not want to compose another *Don Quixote*—
which would be easy—but *the Don Quixote*. It is unnecessary to add that his aim was never to produce a mechanical
transcription of the original; he did not propose to copy it.
His admirable ambition was to produce pages which would

*I also had another, secondary intent—
that of sketching a portrait of Pierre
Menard. But how would I dare to
compete with the golden pages the
Baroness de Bacourt tells me she is
preparing, or with the delicate and
precise pencil of Carolus Hourcade?

coincide—word for word and line for line—with those of
Miguel de Cervantes.

"My intent is merely astonishing," he wrote me from
Bayonne on December 30th, 1934. "The ultimate goal of a
theological or metaphysical demonstration—the external
world, God, chance, universal forms—are no less anterior or
common than this novel which I am now developing. The
only difference is that philosophers publish in pleasant
volumes the intermediary stages of their work and that I
have decided to lose them." And, in fact, not one page of a
rough draft remains to bear witness to this work of years.

The initial method he conceived was relatively simple: to
know Spanish well, to re-embrace the Catholic faith, to fight
against Moors and Turks, to forget European history between 1602 and 1918, and to be Miguel de Cervantes. Pierre
Menard studied this procedure (I know that he arrived
at a rather faithful handling of seventeenth-century Spanish)
but rejected it as too easy. Rather because it was impossible,
the reader will say! I agree, but the undertaking was impossible from the start, and of all the possible means of
carrying it out, this one was the least interesting. To be,
in the twentieth century, a popular novelist of the seventeenth seemed to him a diminution. To be, in some way,
Cervantes and to arrive at *Don Quixote* seemed to him less
arduous—and consequently less interesting—than to continue being Pierre Menard and to arrive at *Don Quixote*
through the experience of Pierre Menard. (This conviction,
let it be said in passing, forced him to exclude the auto-
biographical prologue of the second part of *Don Quixote*.
To include this prologue would have meant creating another personage—Cervantes—but it would also have meant
presenting *Don Quixote* as the work of this personage and
not of Menard. He naturally denied himself such an easy
solution.) "My undertaking is not essentially difficult," I
read in another part of the same letter. "I would only have
to be immortal in order to carry it out." Shall I confess that
I often imagine that he finished it and that I am reading
Don Quixote—the entire work—as if Menard had conceived

it? Several nights ago, while leafing through Chapter XXVI
—which he had never attempted—I recognized our friend's
style and, as it were, his voice in this exceptional phrase:
the nymphs of the rivers, mournful and humid Echo. This
effective combination of two adjectives, one moral and the
other physical, reminded me of a line from Shakespeare
which we discussed one afternoon:

> *Where a malignant and turbaned Turk . . .*

Why precisely *Don Quixote,* our reader will ask. Such a
preference would not have been inexplicable in a Spaniard;
but it undoubtedly was in a symbolist from Nîmes, essentially devoted to Poe, who engendered Baudelaire, who
engendered Mallarmé, who engendered Valéry, who engendered Edmond Teste. The letter quoted above clarifies
this point. *"Don Quixote,"* Menard explains, "interests me
profoundly, but it does not seem to me to have been—how
shall I say it—inevitable. I cannot imagine the universe
without the interjection of Edgar Allen Poe

> *Ah, bear in mind this garden was enchanted!*

or without the *Bateau ivre* or the *Ancient Mariner,* but I
know that I am capable of imagining it without *Don Quixote.*
(I speak, naturally, of my personal capacity, not of the
historical repercussions of these works.) *Don Quixote* is an
accidental book, *Don Quixote* is unnecessary. I can pre-
meditate writing, I can write it, without incurring a tau-
tology. When I was twelve or thirteen years old I read it,
perhaps in its entirety. Since then I have reread several
chapters attentively, but not the ones I am going to undertake. I have likewise studied the *entremeses,* the comedies,
the *Galatea,* the exemplary novels, and the undoubtedly
laborious efforts of *Pérsiles y Sigismunda* and the *Viaje al
Parnaso.* . . . My general memory of *Don Quixote,* simplified
by forgetfulness and indifference, is much the same as the
imprecise, anterior image of a book not yet written. Once
this image (which no one can deny me in good faith) has
been postulated, my problems are undeniably considerably

more difficult than those which Cervantes faced. My affable
precursor did not refuse the collaboration of fate; he went
along composing his immortal work a little *à la diable,*
swept along by inertias of language and invention. I have
contracted the mysterious duty of reconstructing literally
his spontaneous work. My solitary game is governed by two
polar laws. The first permits me to attempt variants of a
formal and psychological nature; the second obliges me to
sacrifice them to the 'original' text and irrefutably to ra-
tionalize this annihilation. . . . To these artificial obstacles
one must add another congenital one. To compose *Don
Quixote* at the beginning of the seventeenth century was a
reasonable, necessary and perhaps inevitable undertaking;
at the beginning of the twentieth century it is almost impossible. It is not in vain that three hundred years have
passed, charged with the most complex happenings—among
them, to mention only one, that same *Don Quixote.*"

In spite of these three obstacles, the fragmentary *Don
Quixote* of Menard is more subtle than that of Cervantes.
The latter indulges in a rather coarse opposition between
tales of knighthood and the meager, provincial reality of
his country; Menard chooses as "reality" the land of Car-
men during the century of Lepanto and Lope. What His-
panophile would not have advised Maurice Barrès or Dr.
Rodríguez Larreta to make such a choice! Menard, as if it
were the most natural thing in the world, eludes them. In
his work there are neither bands of gypsies, conquistadors,
mystics, Philip the Seconds, nor autos-da-fé. He disregards
or proscribes local color. This disdain indicates a new approach to the historical novel. This disdain condemns
Salammbô without appeal.

It is no less astonishing to consider isolated chapters. Let
us examine, for instance, Chapter XXXVIII of Part One
"which treats of the curious discourse that Don Quixote
delivered on the subject of arms and letters." As is known,
Don Quixote (like Quevedo in a later, analogous passage of
La hora de todos) passes judgment against letters and in
favor of arms. Cervantes was an old soldier, which explains

such a judgment. But that the *Don Quixote* of Pierre Menard —a contemporary of *La trahison des clercs* and Bertrand Russell—should relapse into these nebulous sophistries! Madame Bachelier has seen in them an admirable and typical subordination of the author to the psychology of the hero; others (by no means perspicaciously) a *transcription* of *Don Quixote;* the Baroness de Bacourt, the influence of Nietzsche. To this third interpretation (which seems to me irrefutable) I do not know if I would dare to add a fourth, which coincides very well with the divine modesty of Pierre Menard: his resigned or ironic habit of propounding ideas which were the strict reverse of those he preferred. (One will remember his diatribe against Paul Valéry in the ephemeral journal of the superrealist Jacques Reboul.) The text of Cervantes and that of Menard are verbally identical, but the second is almost infinitely richer. (More ambiguous, his detractors will say; but ambiguity is a richness.) It is a revelation to compare the *Don Quixote* of Menard with that of Cervantes. The latter, for instance, wrote (*Don Quixote,* Part One, Chapter Nine):

> . . . *la verdad, cuya madre es la historia, émula del tiempo, depósito de las acciones, testigo de lo pasado, ejemplo y aviso de lo presente, advertencia de lo por venir.*

> [. . . truth, whose mother is history, who is the rival of time, depository of deeds, witness of the past, example and lesson to the present, and warning to the future.]

Written in the seventeenth century, written by the "ingenious layman" Cervantes, this enumeration is a mere rhetorical eulogy of history. Menard, on the other hand, writes:

> . . . *la verdad, cuya madre es la historia, émula del tiempo, depósito de las acciones, testigo de lo pasado, ejemplo y aviso de lo presente, advertencia de lo por venir.*

> [. . . truth, whose mother is history, who is the rival of time, depository of deeds, witness of the past, example and lesson to the present, and warning to the future.]

History, *mother* of truth; the idea is astounding. Menard,

a contemporary of William James, does not define history as an investigation of reality, but as its origin. Historical truth, for him, is not what took place; it is what we think took place. The final clauses—*example and lesson to the present, and warning to the future*—are shamelessly pragmatic.

Equally vivid is the contrast in styles. The archaic style of Menard—in the last analysis, a foreigner—suffers from a certain affectation. Not so that of his precursor, who handles easily the ordinary Spanish of his time.

There is no intellectual exercise which is not ultimately useless. A philosophical doctrine is in the beginning a seemingly true description of the universe; as the years pass it becomes a mere chapter—if not a paragraph or a noun—in the history of philosophy. In literature, this ultimate decay is even more notorious. *"Don Quixote,"* Menard once told me, *"*was above all an agreeable book; now it is an occasion for patriotic toasts, grammatical arrogance and obscene deluxe editions. Glory is an incomprehension, and perhaps the worst."

These nihilist arguments contain nothing new; what is unusual is the decision Pierre Menard derived from them. He resolved to outstrip that vanity which awaits all the woes of mankind; he undertook a task that was complex in the extreme and futile from the outset. He dedicated his conscience and nightly studies to the repetition of a pre-existing book in a foreign tongue. The number of rough drafts kept on increasing; he tenaciously made corrections and tore up thousands of manuscript pages.* He did not permit them to be examined, and he took great care that they would not survive him. It is in vain that I have tried to reconstruct them.

I have thought that it is legitimate to consider the "final" *Don Quixote* as a kind of palimpsest, in which should appear traces—tenuous but not undecipherable—of the "previous"

*I remember his square-ruled notebooks, the black streaks where he had crossed out words, his peculiar typographical symbols and his insect-like handwriting. In the late afternoon he liked to go for walks on the outskirts of Nîmes; he would take a notebook with him and make a gay bonfire.

handwriting of our friend. Unfortunately, only a second
Pierre Menard, inverting the work of the former, could
exhume and resuscitate these Troys. . . .

"To think, analyze and invent," he also wrote me, "are
not anomalous acts, but the normal respiration of the intelligence. To glorify the occasional fulfillment of this function,
to treasure ancient thoughts of others, to remember with
incredulous amazement that the *doctor universalis* thought,
is to confess our languor or barbarism. Every man should
be capable of all ideas, and I believe that in the future he
will be."

Menard (perhaps without wishing to) has enriched, by
means of a new technique, the hesitant and rudimentary
art of reading; the technique is one of deliberate anachronism
and erroneous attributions. This technique, with its infinite
applications, urges us to run through the *Odyssey* as if it
were written after the *Aeneid,* and to read *Le jardin du
Centaure* by Madame Henri Bachelier as if it were by
Madame Henri Bachelier. This technique would fill the
dullest books with adventure. Would not the attributing of
The Imitation of Christ to Louis Ferdinand Céline or James
Joyce be a sufficient renovation of its tenuous spiritual
counsels?

—Jorge Luis Borges
—Translated by Anthony Bonner

The Romantic Triumph:
The Warp and the Wolf

He who laughs least lasts best.

—Shakespeare

∽ With the publication of *Lyrical Ballast* William Wordsworth assumed the chief position in English letters formally
held by Dr. Johnson. Born in London, Wordsworth spent
his childhood near the Great Lakes, among the Wiggles-
worths, Wordsworths, and Woolworths of Wordsworthshire.
Later he attended Maudlin College, Oxford, where he invented
perpetual emotion in his "Lines Composed near Northanger
Abbey." Flowers violently affected a man of Wordsworth's
constituency—especially cauliflowers, dactyls, and never-
greens—and even the meanest flower that blows brought
him thoughts which lay, fortunately, too deep for tears.
Following his marriage he assumed the name of "Daddy
Wordsworth" and speedily became one of England's most
prolific writers.

Wordsworth frequently wrote poems and prefaces, and
sometimes he wrote literature. His most famous mistake
appeared in "The Solitary Raper," composed by the seaside
near Cathay: "The child," he wrote, "is the father of the
man." He was particularly proud of his "Ode on Imitations
of Immorality from Regulations of Early Childhood," in
which he maintained that rural life is found chiefly in the

country. His pathetic fallacy was, of course, his persistence in writing poetry even after his inspiration had ceased.

William Jennings Byron, author of "Thanatopsis," is considered "the playboy of the western world." As a child he was called Harold, but at school he became known as the Wolf. At Harrow he played Rugby, served on the tennis team, and gambled on the village green with Bella Donna, an Italian lady of English distraction. Finally he married his first cousin, and the belles of London peeled forth. After that first fine careless rupture, however, the Byrons moved from Bond Street to Tobacco Road, where Lord Byron lived amid all the unadulterated lust practicable in a private household. On the morning after the appearance of *English Birds and Scotch Retrievers* he awoke to find himself, but was disappointed. Later he was exiled to Don Juan, whence he finally escaped to Greece. In Athens he visited the Palace Athena, the Pantheon, and the Apocalypse, and there, amid the throws of a wild and wolfy love affair, he was inspired to compose "Child Harold to the Dark Tower Came." After numerous touching scenes he died in the Battle of Marathon. Psychiatrists now believe that Byron suffered from lycanthropy, according to which one is cracked (symmetrically) and imagines himself to be and acts like a wolf. Certainly his sounding brass and tinkling symbols reveal a man less sinned against than sinning, but he was probably a good man underneath. His poetry embraces all mankind—especially persons of the opposite sex.

Most fragile of all romantic poets was Percy Bysshe Shelley, a victim of abnormal psychology, whom Benedict Arnold once called "an ineffective Anglican flapping his lunatic wings in the void." Shelley's poetry may be termed "strictly platonic," but his private life found best expression in *Promiscuous Unbound,* a tragedy based on the philosophy of Plato and Isosceles. His belief in Pantherism first appeared in "Adenoids," a lament for Keats based on Byron's "Lament for Adonais." Unfortunately Shelley died while drowning in the Bay of Spumoni. A simple epithet marks his tomb: "Here lies one whose fame was writ in water."

In his "Ode on a Greasy Urn" John Keats proved himself the most sensual poet in the language. At twenty-five
he married a musician named Agnes Dei, and on top of
that he met a speedy death from tuberoses. Keats' wife
inspired "The Keats of St. Agnes," a narrative poem dedicated to Calliope, Errata, and Uranium. But his greatest
contribution to English literature is his "Ode to Madame
Nightingale," addressed to the famous French opera singer
who, filled with the milk of human kindness, nursed to
health the British soldiers of the Crimean War.

—Robert Manson Myers

The Transcendentalists

⌒ After Irving, Cooper, and Bryant, the literary center of the United States moved from New York to New England. On Moving Day, roads were clogged with hundreds of poets, novelists, essayists, and editors, loaded down with the tools of their trade.[1]

The Transcendentalists were a group of New Englanders who looked upon themselves as mystics and were looked upon by others as queer. They formed a club, originally called the Aesthetic Club, or possibly Anaesthetic Club, where they sat around and talked about Immanuel Kant.[2] "I believe there was seldom an inclination to be silent," said one of the members. This is a Bostonian's way of saying that everybody talked at once.

One practical result of discussions at the Club was establishment of Brook Farm, a socialistic community where agriculture and the arts mingled, it being common practice to milk a cow with one hand while painting a landscape or writing a poem with the other. Mostly, however, unpleasant chores were assigned to a committee and forgotten, life being so beautiful that everyone was too busy looking at it to work. Despite emphasis on the individual, there was belief in mutual helpfulness. It was, as Emerson said, "an attempt to lift others with themselves." The sight of a Brook farmer struggling to lift himself with one hand and a friend with the other sometimes startled passersby.

[1] Pens, erasers, paperweights, and rejection slips.

[2] "If Kant can't, nobody can," they were wont to say admiringly.

Ralph Waldo Emerson

The leader of the Transcendentalists was Ralph Waldo Emerson. Ralph (as few dared call him) came of a long line of Puritan ministers, which explains a great deal. He himself was a preacher for a while, and even after he left the pulpit continued preaching, as anyone knows who has read his essays.

Emerson lived most of his life in Boston and in Concord. In the latter he occupied a house that had been built for his grandfather and was therefore referred to as "the Old Man's."[3] It was there that Emerson wrote his book *Nature*, which is about nature. There too, during a heavy rainstorm, he made his famous pronouncement: "Nature is not fixed but fluid."

A versatile writer, Emerson wrote both prose and poetry. It has been said that there are poetic passages in his prose and prosaic passages in his poetry. No doubt he did this on purpose, to confound his critics.[4] However, his poetry can easily be distinguished, even when it is not distinguished poetry, by such lines as:

> I like a church; I like a cowl;
> I love a prophet of the soul.

If you mispronounce either *cowl* or *soul*, but not both, it rhymes perfectly.

Many of Emerson's essays were first delivered as lectures. These lectures (for which he was well paid—see his essay "Compensation") took him all over the United States and to Europe. In England he was entertained by famous writers. One of them, George Eliot, jotted this somewhat cryptic entry in her diary: "He is the first *man* I have ever met." She was living at the time with George Henry Lewes, and it is a good thing she kept the key to her diary on a string around her neck.[5]

[3] Mistakenly referred to today as the Old Manse.

[4] "Confound my critics!" Emerson often said.

[5] George Eliot, it should be noted, was *not* a man.

Emerson has been described as "a deep-seated genius," which is the kind of remark about a writer's physical appearance that a literary critic should never make. It would be kinder to say something about his Over-Soul, which might have been big and baggy but didn't show.[6]

In his essays,[7] Emerson urges reliance on self, which he refers to as Self-Reliance. In fact self was so important to him that when he traveled in Europe he wrote in his journal, after a hard day's sightseeing, "Wherever we go, whatever we do, self is the sole subject we study and learn." Some think he might have saved all that money and stayed home.

Anyone who has difficulty understanding Emerson will be helped by the following explanation: "The Kantian tripartition supplied the epistemological terminology for Emersonian transcendentalism." Suddenly it all becomes clear.

Henry David Thoreau

The No. 2 Transcendentalist, whose number was up before Emerson's (he lived to be only forty-five), was Henry David Thoreau.[8] Thoreau grew up in Concord, where his father was a manufacturer of lead pencils. Since the youth could have all the rejects that couldn't be sold, it is no wonder he became a writer.

Rather than earn money, it was Thoreau's idea to reduce his wants so that he would not need to buy anything. As he went around town preaching this ingenious idea, the shopkeepers of Concord hoped he would drop dead. Nor did his refusal to pay taxes endear him to local officials. Shuddering at the prospect of having a crank like Thoreau in the county jail, always demanding his special health-food diet, they paid his taxes and considered themselves fortunate.

Thoreau built himself a cabin on the shores of Walden

---

[6] Or did it? Emerson himself refers to the Over-Soul as "the lap of immense intelligence."

[7] Entitled, with Emerson's customary flair for the unusual, *Essays, First Series* and *Essays, Second Series*.

[8] At first his name was David Henry Thoreau, but apparently he got himself mixed up.

Pond, near Concord, at a cost of $28.12½.[9] At least that is
what he told the county tax assessor when he came to
appraise the place. Thoreau was his own architect, carpenter, plasterer, and electrician, and he did without plumbing.[10]

Why Thoreau went to live alone at Walden, where he
stayed two years and two months, he once explained as
follows: "I wanted to live deep and suck out all the marrow
of life." The picture of this rugged individualist crouched in
a hole he had dug near his cabin, working away on a bone,
is likely to linger for many a day.

Emerson, who enjoyed comfort, wrote of Thoreau somewhat irascibly: "I tell him a man was not made to live in
a swamp, but a frog. If God meant him to live in a swamp,
he would have made him a frog." Thoreau, who loved frogs
just as he did ants and beetles, accepted this as a compli-
ment and on summer evenings took to croaking softly.

Out of his experiences Thoreau wrote *Walden,* which
hymns the pleasures of being alone with nature—away from
newspapers, telephones, and Ralph Waldo Emerson. "If the
bell rings, why should we run?" asks Thoreau. Callers who
knocked on the door of his cabin often went away, thinking
he was not home. Actually, he was getting out of his chair,
but slowly.

It is probably unnecessary to say that Thoreau, preoc-
cupied with eliminating what he called "superfluities," never
married.[11]

Other Transcendentalists

Other Transcendentalists included Orestes Brownson, who,
fortunately, was not on a first-name basis with many persons,
and Bronson Alcott. Alcott founded Fruitlands, an experiment in vegetarian living, which broke up after a few months.

[9] Thoreau not only cut corners, he cut
pennies.

[10] There were woods all around the
place.

[11] "As for taking Henry's arm," said one
of his friends, "I should as soon think of
taking the arm of an elm tree." Thoreau
was a lovable fellow, but there was
something a little wooden about him.

One night at dinner, when the Fruitlanders were eating squash and turnip greens for the fourteenth time that week, the scent of roast beef drifted in from a neighboring farmhouse.

With the failure of Fruitlands, Alcott was in financial straits, but, being a man of high ideals, he refused to permit just anyone to support him. Almost the only person who passed his rigorous standards was his daughter, Louisa May Alcott, who had made a fortune with her *Little Women,* a sweet tearful saga of four sisters.[12]

There was also Margaret Fuller, whom the male Transcendentalists accepted as an intellectual equal. Fortunately for her, these eccentrics were more interested in brains than beauty. As editor of the Transcendentalist publication, the *Dial,* she displayed a blend of idealism and practicality by paying nothing to its contributors. Of course, the fact that the paid circulation of the *Dial* never exceeded 250 may have limited her funds.

—Richard Armour

[12] The term *sob sister* was first applied to Beth and her damp siblings.

Thomas Mann and Eighteenth-Century Comic Fiction

∽ All my life I have been extremely careful to avoid the pitfalls into which I have observed my associates falling. I perhaps need offer no more compelling evidence of this care than my procedure when I came to write my Ph.D. dissertation. All around me I saw graduate students getting into difficulties with their dissertations. Some of them were choosing authors whom everyone thought to be insignificant, and trying their best, against all odds, to make them significant. Others were choosing authors whom everyone recognized to be great—I mention only Shakespeare—and trying to find something fresh to be said on a subject already exhausted. I of course took the middle path: I chose to write on a figure who was unquestionably the greatest in his genre, but who had never been given his full measure of praise. The choice made, I then carefully avoided other pitfalls: I did not try to treat my man exhaustively, or even originally, as some of my more reckless companions were attempting to do with their men. Rather I limited myself to what my thesis chairman liked to call a "negotiable scope." Though it was clear to me that *Tristram Shandy* was the greatest novel ever written, I did not try to establish that point—a task that could easily have taken a full year to complete. Instead, I made a simple and cogent study of Laurence Sterne's journey to Toulouse (*via* Auxerre, Lyons, Avignon,

and Montpellier) during the winter of 1763.[1] I did not even
try to establish that this period was the turning point in
Sterne's career; I was content to show—and no one has as
yet seen fit to attempt a refutation—that this visit is reflected
quite clearly in *Tristram Shandy,* Volume III, Chapter xxvii,
and again, though perhaps less clearly, in Volume VIII,
Chapter xxx. As a result of this modesty—I might even say
integrity—of aims, I finished my degree before any one of my
contemporaries in the English department, except my close
friend who, sacrificing quality to speed, was content to do a
study of the critical reputation of Beroalde de Verville in
America during the nineteenth century. Since no one in
America had ever mentioned this follower of Rabelais until
twentieth-century scholars noticed him apropos of *Tristram
Shandy,* my friend's conclusions were largely negative, and
the whole job took him just under three months, two of
which were spent in supervising the typing and proofreading.

I mention all this to make credible what I can now only
call my blind caution in my first productive scholarship
after the degree was conferred. With my usual prudence, I
had looked ahead to discover what errors my colleagues were
inclined to commit in the years of work left to them when
they were once free. It will be no surprise to my readers,
if they are at all familiar with academic pursuits, to learn
that the most frequent and fatal error was dissertation
riding. The annals of *PMLA*[2] are filled with the names of
scholars who have spent their lives developing the claims
they staked with their dissertations. I perhaps need mention
only Dr. F. M. Q____, who earned his degree with a study
of Giles Fletcher, the younger (1588?-1623). He of course
discovered that Fletcher was much more important than
anyone had ever before realized, since, contrary to all previous opinion, he wrote two plays in addition to his poems:
Emunctories Cleansèd, A Masque, and *In Praise of Fools,*
a dramatization of Erasmus's *Encomium Moriae.* These

---

[1] Wilbur L. Cross, *The Life and Times*   [2] *PMLA, Annals, passim.*
of Laurence Sterne (New York, 1929),
p. 660.

plays, he found, were really the finest artistic flowering of
Fletcher's whole period, being in reality the models aimed
at (and sometimes indeed surpassed) by Shakespeare in his
last period.[3] The dissertation finished and tucked away in
the stacks, he began to read, for the first time in many
years, literature written after 1623. He found that everybody
who wrote plays after Giles Fletcher, the younger, was
influenced by him much more than the scholarly world
had ever suspected. He read Otway, and to him Otway
seemed merely the Restoration Fletcher. He discovered
that *George Barnwell, The Cenci,* Dickens's and Collins's
No Thoroughfare, A Drama, Wilde's *The Duchess of Padua:*   .
A Tragedy of the XVI Century, and, among other modern
plays, *A Streetcar Named Desire*—these and many others
he found derived either their dramatic form or their more
important representational devices, or, in a surprising number of cases, both, from Fletcher. He quite naturally began
to write and publish essays about his discoveries and before
he was aware of what had happened, he had collected the
essays, published over a twenty-year period, under the title
Giles Fletcher and his Followers: The Great Tradition.
Upon his retirement, his students and colleagues considered
putting together a memorial volume of his critical essays
over four decades, but they were so embarrassed by the
monotony of the subject, and the monomania of its treatment that they abandoned the project. He did not get his
memorial volume!

To see this happen to only one man would have been
sufficient warning to me. But to see the same kind of wasted
life result for one after another of those who failed to see
their man in the context of the whole made me determined
to get away from Sterne the day after graduation, and to
stay away. I was of course aware of a strong tradition of
belief in Sterne as a powerful influence; I had read essays
on "Sterne and Jean Paul," "Sterne und Goethe," "Sterne
and C. M. Wieland," "Laurence Sterne und Wilhelm Raahe,"

[3] The plays were written when Fletcher
was a very young man.

"Sterne et William Combe," and "Sterne and Lord Aboyne."
But although some of the evidence offered in these articles,
qua evidence, seemed quite sound, I was not in the least
tempted to abandon my caution. In fact, painful as it now
is to admit it, I refused to see Sterne's influence anywhere.
As I began my first reading beyond 1767 in five years, I
systematically blinded myself to any evidence that might
have indicated that Sterne was anything more, to borrow
a phrase from the great George Saintsbury, than just another
one of the "four wheels of the novel wain," the other three
being of course Richardson, Fielding, and Smollett.[4] When I
heard of *The Life and Opinions of Miss Sukey Shandy of
Bow Street, Gentlewoman, in a Series of Letters to her
Dear Brother, Tristram Shandy, Gent.,* I of course recognized
the similiarity of the names, but I did not leap to the
assumption that this was a Shandean imitation. Rather,
I took pains: I obtained a photostatic copy from the British
Museum. The book did indeed resemble *Tristram Shandy*
rather strongly, but, incredible as it now seems, I was able
to convince myself that the resemblances were really due
to the author's borrowing rather heavily from authors whom
Sterne had borrowed from: Beroalde de Verville, Bruscambille,
and others. Similarly, I refused to believe, what everyone
now accepts, that *A Supplement to the Life and Opinions
of Tristram Shandy* (1761) was directly inspired by *Tristram
Shandy* itself.

It should not be hard to understand that with such an
attitude I was not converted easily to recognizing Sterne's
true influence. It happened only gradually and would never
have happened at all if I had not decided to leave the
eighteenth century, and, for the first time since entering
graduate school, read a modern novel. In one graduate
course Joyce's *Ulysses* had been praised, with a boldness
not often encountered in graduate school, as a "pivotal"
modern work. Since I was determined to read nothing
but pivotal works, I began to read *Ulysses.*

[4] George Saintsbury, *The English Novel,*
p. 320.

Even then, even on first reading—even before I so much as suspected what I know now—I felt—I'm sure that I can remember feeling—an uneasy conviction that I was encountering echoes of Sterne. These were nothing like my earlier suspicions, so easily put down, about *Sukey Shandy* and *A Supplement to Tristram Shandy*. I *knew* I had something that I could not ignore. Joyce's deliberate attempt to maintain a consecutive story on several levels at once—the elaborate play between actual duration and poetic duration—the use of stream-of-consciousness (a term which at that time was unknown to me, although the phenomenon was clear even without a name)—all seemed—and I tremble even now to remember the confusion in my heart as I saw the dangerous and exciting new territory opening before me—all seemed fairly obvious imitations of Tristramshandeism.

Of course I was still cautious: I said nothing. Even when, with Molly's final yes, the total picture of Joyce's attempt became clear to me and I became absolutely convinced, I still demurred. I hid the book behind my five-volume illustrated set of the complete works of Bruscambille, including the "Prologue on Long Noses" mentioned by Sterne, and tried to forget. But one day as I was sitting in my office reading *Farrago,* by Pilgrim Plowden, Esquire (London, 17—), an academic friend—one of those who can never let another man's man alone—came to me with a copy of *James Joyce: Two Decades of Criticism.*

"This should interest you," he said, thrusting the book on my desk before me, opened to page twelve. It was a bit of reminiscence by Eugène Jolas:

> It is not very difficult to follow a simple, chronological scheme which the critics will understand [Joyce was saying to him] . . . But I, after all, am trying to tell the story of this Chapelizod family in a new way . . . Only I am trying to build many planes of narrative with a single esthetic purpose. . . . Did you ever read Laurence Sterne . . . ?

I am afraid I lost my head. I plunged homeward, trying to remember what role a Chapelizod family had played in *Ulysses.* I flung the Bruscambille from the shelf, snatched down *Ulysses,* raced through it—and found nothing. I hurried back to school, and read Jolas's passage again, finally studying the context. It was explicitly, as I should have noticed from the beginning, a reference to *Work in Progress,* now known as *Finnegans Wake,* rather than to *Ulysses.* For the moment I did not know quite what to do with this confusing detail. That *Finnegans Wake* is an imitation of *Tristram Shandy* was perhaps a useful discovery, but my original feeling had been inspired by *Ulysses,* and it was evidence about *Ulysses* for which I thirsted. To those who thirst will drink be given,[5] and I finally found what I desired, a statement in *Le livre jaune* (August, 1945) to the effect that *Finnegans Wake* was simply the logical development of tendencies to be discovered in *all* of Joyce's earlier work. It followed that anything *Finnegans Wake* was, *Ulysses* was, and my original feeling was now demonstrated to have been sound.

Well, I wrote my article. *"Tristram Shandy, Ulysses,* and *Finnegans Wake,"* I called it, with what still seems to me admirable restraint. Much to my surprise, the editor of *Modern Philology,* to whom I sent the piece, scribbled "Oh, come now!" on the title page and sent it back. At first I thought he had had some difficulty following the argument, which indeed was occasionally somewhat rarefied: I had had to abandon the reading of *Finnegans Wake* after several attempts, so that my *arguments* were all about *Finnegans Wake* and my *evidence* was all drawn from *Ulysses.* But I am now convinced that the editor had read only the title page. It was of course a mistake to have given away in the title the full force of my break with tradition. I have since learned better rhetorical techniques (cf. my present title), and have some reason to believe that at least one editor read more than one-third of one article I sent him (there was a "God!" penciled in the margin on page 35) although like all the others he did not print what I had to offer. But I am getting ahead of my story.

[5] *Guide to Research in English Literature,*
5th ed., 1950, article on "Thirst."

In spite of editorial indifference, I was on fire; I knew instinctively that my discoveries had just begun. Yet I was determined to move slowly and with caution: I read another pivotal work, *A la recherche du temps perdu* (In Remembrance of Things Past). As soon as I saw that it was narrated in the first person, I knew that my choice had been justified. And when I finished reading, three months later, there was nothing to do but write another article—or I should say Chapter—"Proust and Sterne," in which I argued, quite simply, that *Tristram Shandy* is the *comic* story of a narrator writing a book, and *A la recherche du temps perdu* is a *serious* story of a narrator writing a book. Proust's so-called originality consists in nothing more than adapting Sterne's suggestion to a different kind of narrator: the hypersensitive, pathetically isolated genius-type. The body of the paper demonstrated the chapter-by-chapter parallelism, in too great detail to allow for reproduction here. I need only say that it has been called by at least one Sterne scholar, to whom I showed the manuscript, a model of deductive scholarship.[6]

Now to understand my situation at this point it will be necessary to recapitulate briefly. I had read a total of two modern novels. Both of them were rated as pivotal, yet both of them had proved to be hardly more than third-rate extensions of techniques magnificently originated by Sterne. Nevertheless, cautious as always, I refused to generalize without further evidence. I chose another pivot: Gide. Eduard's journal in *Les faux-monnayeurs* proved of course to be nothing but a *serious* condensation of Sterne's *comic*

---

[6] The reader may well wonder why I did not wait for some external evidence of the compelling kind I had previously discovered about Joyce. Needless to say, I searched for whatever could be found, but there was nothing. I knew a girl who was compiling an index of names occurring in all of Proust's works. She told me that neither *Sterne* nor *Shandy* was in her index. I asked her what about *Tristram,* under the T's, but for simplicity she had indexed everyone under his last name: Lescaut (Manon); Dick (Moby); etc. I felt that my internal evidence was really strong enough to make further search for external evidence a work of supererogation, and consequently my failure did not disturb me. It was, incidentally, only after my work on Gide that I began to understand the true significance of Proust's silence about Sterne (see below).

digressions on his art. As soon as it became perfectly obvious
to me that Gide was simply copying Sterne, I did not even
bother to finish the novel, but began to look around for some
external proof, for those readers (and editors) who might
object if I duplicated my exclusively *aesthetic* treatment
of Proust. I leafed through the *Journal des faux-monnayeurs*.
To my surprise, Sterne was not mentioned as one of Gide's
models. I decided that I must work with more subtlety. I
said to myself: "If *you* were writing an imitation of Sterne,
would you mention Sterne, in a journal describing your
writing methods? Of course not. You would mention, as
Gide does, Proust, Stendhal, Dickens, Dostoievski, Tolstoy—
anyone *but* Sterne."

That this approach was sound was shown when I read
through *all* the journals. I discovered the first explicit
reference to Sterne in Gide's entry for April 23, 1932, where
he quotes, with seeming unconcern, from *Tristram Shandy,*
obviously striving to indicate that he is reading the book for
the first time. Certainly this is one of the shrewdest moves
ever undertaken by a novelist desiring to cover his tracks.
Gide pretends to be reading *Tristram Shandy* for the first
time, *six years after* his own imitation was published. Now
it is certainly not to my purpose to attack Gide here; it is
enough if the reader recognize that Gide even more clearly
than Joyce openly betrays that he owes everything to Sterne.
That he somewhat ungraciously disguises the avowal may
make us think less of him as a *man* (and by the same token
more of Joyce), but it does not affect the quality either of
his novels as imitations of Sterne, or of my argument.

It was only now, having encountered Gide's deceptiveness,
that I was able properly to evaluate Proust's silence concerning Sterne. One need only consider the number of pages which
Proust wrote, in his novels, his newspaper sketches and
reviews, his letters, and his journals, to realize the enormity
of the revelation he makes of his own plagiary in never
mentioning, on any one of those thousands of pages, the
man who was not only the greatest novelist of all time,
but the man who of all other writers had the greatest in-

fluence on Proust. Again I do not wish to indulge in unpleasant talk about the morality of men whose works, since they embody principles discovered by Sterne, I admire. Yet one can hardly refrain from comparing Sterne's open-hearted confessions of indebtedness to Rabelais, Cervantes, Swift, Montaigne, etc., with the awful silence of Proust.

But I digress. It was clear to me now that I must begin to protect myself. I already had a book on my hands, *Tristram Shandy, the Father of the Modern Novel,* and if I maintained my one-hundred per cent average, it would be a trilogy within a year. Yet it was equally clear that since no one had been willing to publish any part of my discoveries as yet, no one *would* publish the book unless I took pains to clear myself of any charges of bias. What was worse, my own fears of dissertation riding were as strong as ever. Had I really been working honestly? Was not my growing conviction that *all* modern fiction depended from Sterne a sign that I had fallen into the very error I had been so anxious to avoid?

Clearly the thing to do was to look for an undeniable exception, in order to be able to moderate my claims, for the sake of my own peace of mind and my reputation for objectivity. But if everything was to turn out to be Shandean, how was I to find an exception, without expending several years of my life in the search? I thought at first that some reference work would give me the help I needed. But a hasty survey of the titles I had copied years before in Research Methods 301 convinced me that only a personal interview with a man of wide *modern* scholarship would yield the answer I desired. The question was: Who?

That I did not think of the solution sooner I can only attribute to my graduate training. Contempt for little magazines had been carefully nurtured in us from the start, and it was only with effort that I could bring myself to realize that the very fountainhead of knowledge about modern literature must be the little magazine editor. But when, by dint of sheer ratiocination, I finally came to the truth, I acted swiftly. I inquired, and discovered that the only little magazine edited in my vicinity was *Boom*. I went to the editor of *Boom* and asked him, after appropriate introductions, which of all the great modern novelists was least likely to be a mere imitator of Sterne. He answered without hesitation.

"Thomas Mann is *der Mensch*. I would risk my international reputation as *redacteur* of *Boom* on the categorical assertion that Thomas Mann has never lifted a line from *Tristram Shandy*. Trivia would not interest Thomas Mann. Thomas Mann is an artist *sans peur et sans reproche*."

"What has he written?"

He blanched.

"You ask what Thomas Mann has written? You have not read *Boom's* Memorial Issue? Thomas Mann has written, in chronological order, *The Beloved Returns, Buddenbrooks, Joseph and his Brothers* (consisting of *The Tales of Jacob, Young—*)"

"But," I interrupted, "you do not understand about the disciplines of productive scholarship. You read everything. I want to read—when, as now, I am out of my beloved decade—1757–1767—only the *right* thing. Please forget the *corpus*. Tell me only which of all the titles you have named or could name, which *one* is least likely to have been influenced by Laurence Sterne."

He hesitated.

"If none of them is an imitation, how can there be a question of degree? However, if you merely want to know which of all Mann's works you, in your—ah—enthusiasm, could not claim for Sterne, perhaps I can help." And he began to mumble. *"Death in Venice?* . . . No, there is a digression which might be mistaken . . . *The Magic Mountain?* . . . No, the experience with Madame Chauchat and the pencil might be mistaken for Shandean bawdry . . ."

I waited for perhaps fifteen minutes as he read through them all. At last he smiled.

"None of them, as I said, has *anything* to do with *Tristram Shandy*. But there is only one, the newest one, that I can really trust *you* to read without making ridiculous

discoveries. It is an adaptation of the Faustus legend, which, by the way, Sterne never touched. If it does not serve, nothing will. Mann is the least Shandean of modern authors; *Dr. Faustus*—for that is its name—is the least Shandean of his books. If, to save you from—ah—*vos critiques fâcheuses* and from yourself, you must find an Anti-Tristramshandy, *Dr. Faustus* is my recommendation."

I read it.

That is, I started to read it. I started to read it, and in the first paragraph found Serenus Zeitblom, Ph.D., the narrator, saying:

> I intrude myself, of course, only in order that the reader—I might better say the future reader, for at this moment there exists not the smallest prospect that my manuscript will ever see the light. . . . Indeed, my mind misgives me that I shall only be awakening the reader's doubt whether he is in the right hands: whether, I mean, my whole existence does not disqualify me for the task dictated by my heart rather than by any true competence for the work.

My heart pounded, and not without reason. This was the most deliberate, undisguised borrowing from Sterne I had yet encountered. I went on, of course—I went on and found scarcely a transition, scarcely a narrative device, not taken from Sterne's pen. Not only is the narrator, like Tristram, careful to set himself up as self-conscious about his devices—and secretly master of them—but he is always copying explicit tricks of Sterne's narrative manner:

> Here I break off, chagrined by a sense of my artistic shortcomings and lack of self-control. . . .

It is all there. The reader is brought on the stage and asked to watch the writer at his desk, going through his antics, making his digressions, getting involved in the complexities of his material, masterfully coming through in spite of all obstacles.

> I am entirely aware that with the above paragraph I have again regrettably overweighted this chapter which I had quite intended to keep short. I would not even suppress my suspicion, held on psychological grounds, that

> I actually seek digressions and circumlocutions . . . because
> I am afraid of what is coming. . . . I herewith resume my
> narrative. . . .

But I could go on with these quotations indefinitely.
Indeed, when I came to write up my discovery, I found that
I was able to quote exactly *two-thirds* of the original text
in support of my argument, surely ample proof in itself,
aside from the high *quality* of my evidence, that Mann's
work is simply another avatar of *Tristram Shandy*. I am
tempted to quote almost as largely from these proofs here,
because it is at this point that my case in all its fullness
either stands or falls. But perhaps one splendid example
will have to do: the beginning of Chapter IX, where Mann
avows his debt explicitly. In case this quotation looks too
formidably long for the readers of *Furioso,* who, like all
readers of literature outside the eighteenth century, are
accustomed to being, as one might say, spoon fed, I shall
underline the most significant sections (italics mine):

> And so, half jestingly, I would address those who in
> that last monstrous chapter have been guilty of some
> skipping: *I would remind them of how Laurence Sterne
> once dealt with an imaginary listener* who betrayed
> that she had not always been paying attention. The
> author sent her back to an earlier chapter to fill in the
> gaps in her knowledge. After having informed herself,
> the lady rejoins the group of listeners and is given a
> hearty welcome.
>
> The passage came to my mind because Adrian as a top-
> form student, at the time when I had already left for
> the University of Giessen, studied English outside the
> school courses, and after all outside the humanistic cur-
> riculum, under the influence of Wendell Kretschmar. *He
> read Sterne with great pleasure.* Even more enthusiastical-
> ly he read Shakespeare. . . .

I did not read further, except to look at the first paragraph
of the Epilogue:

> It is finished. An old man, bent, well-nigh broken by
> the horrors of the times in which he wrote. . . . A task
> has been mastered, for which by nature I was not the
> man. . . . In actual fact I have sometimes pondered ways

and means of sending these pages to America, in order
that they might first be laid before the public in an
English translation.....[7]

No, I did not read further. My case—the case I had not
wanted to make, the case for Sterne as the father of all
modern literature—was so firmly established that I did not
need to read further. Mann, the last resort of my doubts,
the last hope of my desire to limit myself to a negotiable
scope, had been found to be as derivative as all the others.

There is little point in reporting on my further, and, as
appears now, final steps. I read a little in Henry James, not
really out of any doubt as to what I should find, but simply
to make my case complete. It is unnecessary to report on
what I discovered about the narrator in such works as *Daisy
Miller, The Author of Beltraffio,* or *The Aspern Papers*—to
say nothing of the longer works—because those of my readers
who have read them with any perception, and *me* with any
sympathy, will already have seen who James's inspiration was,
and those readers who are still holding out are undoubtedly
so committed to the belief that all great works are, as they
are so fond of saying, *sui generis,* that nothing, not even
the most rigorous scientific proof, could convince them of
any further instance of Sterne's universal influence.

I, on the contrary, have now adopted without reservation
the belief that all modern literature is essentially one, that
not only is it *not sui generis,* but it has *one* source and
fountainhead: *TRISTRAM SHANDY.* All literary works
written since Sterne—novels, plays, poems—exist, for me, now,
simultaneously. Indeed, it is to me as if *all* literature except
Tristram Shandy had been written in 1768, the year following the publication of Sterne's final volume. Only dull readers
will be surprised at that word "all." For why, if my discoveries are sound, should I limit their application to works
written after Sterne? If Sterne is the fountainhead of all
modern literature, is he not also the culminating receptacle

[7] As *I* look back on what I have written,
I sometimes think I shall have it translated into Latin, in order that it might
first be published in a language fit for
timeless scholarship.

of all previous developments? Indeed, who, having followed me through this account, can question the essential conservatism of my claim that in this sense every Western writer (for I am not, at least as yet, ready to include any other than the Western tradition) before Sterne was but preparing the way, proclaiming to benighted times fragments of the Truth which was to come? And if this is true, is it not safe to say (borrowing a phrase from the Stagyrite) that *Tristram Shandy* is the "Final Cause" of all Western Literature? It is with this aspect of my discoveries that my decology, on which I am now putting the finishing touches, is to deal. I am still looking for a title, but although it seems to suggest a less sweeping claim than I have in mind, I have tentatively settled on *Laurence Sterne, from Homer to Hemingway: A Study in Influence.* After all, there is no harm, I believe, at this stage of my inquiries, in maintaining an air of restraint.

—Wayne Booth

Poets and Pedants

>>>>>>>>>>>>>>>>>>>>>>>>>>>>

How to Criticize a Poem

1.

∾ I propose to examine the following poem:

> Thirty days hath September,
> April, June, and November:
> All the rest have thirty-one,
> Excepting February alone,
> Which has only eight and a score
> Till leap-year gives it one day more.

2.

The previous critics who have studied this poem, Coleridge among them, have failed to explain what we may describe as its fundamental *dynamic*. This I now propose to do. The first thing to observe is the order in which the names (or verbal constructs) of the months are presented. According to the prose meaning—what I shall henceforth call the prose-*demand*—"September" should not precede, it should follow "April," as a glance at the calendar will show. Indeed "September" should follow not only "April," it should also follow "June" if the prose-demand is to be properly satisfied. The prose order of the first two lines should therefore read: "Thirty days hath April, June, September, and November." That is the only sequence consonant with prose logic.

3.

Why then, we ask ourselves, did the poet violate what educated readers know to be the facts? Was he ignorant of the calendar, believing that September preceded April in the progress of the seasons? It is difficult to imagine that such was the case. We must find another explanation. It is here that the principle of dynamic analysis comes to our aid.

4.

Dynamic analysis proves that the most successful poetry achieves its effect by producing an *expectation* in the reader's mind before his sensibility is fully prepared to receive the full impact of the poem. The reader makes a *proto-response* which preconditions him to the total response toward which his fully equilibrized organs of apperception subconsciously tend. It is this proto-response which the poet has here so sensitively manipulated. The ordinary reader, trained only to prose-demands, expects the usual order of the months. But the poet's sensibility knows that poetic truth is more immediately effective than the truth of literal chronology. He does not *state* the inevitable sequence; he *prepares* us for it. In his profound analysis of the two varieties of mensual time, he puts the *gentlest* month first. (Notice how the harsh sound of "pt" in "September" is softened by the "e" sound on either side of it.) It is the month in which vegetation first begins to fade, but which does not as yet give us a sense of tragic fatality.

5.

Hence the poet prepares us, dynamically, for what is to follow. By beginning his list of the months *in medias res,* he is enabled to return later to the beginning of the series of contrasts which is the subject of his poem. The analogy to the "Oedipus Rex" of Euripides and the "Iliad" of Dante at once becomes clear. Recent criticism has only too often failed to observe that these works also illustrate the dynamic method by beginning in the middle of things. It is a striking fact, hitherto (I believe) unnoticed, that a Latin poem called the "Aeneid" does much the same thing. We expect the author of that poem to begin with the departure of his hero from Troy, just as we expect the author of our poem to begin with "April." But in neither case is our expectation fulfilled. Cato, the author of the "Aeneid," creates dynamic suspense by beginning with Aeneas in Carthage; our anonymous poet treats his readers' sensibilities in a similar fashion by beginning with "September," and then *going back* to "April" and "June."

6.

But the sensibility of the poet does not stop at this point. Having described what is true of *four* months, he disposes of *seven* more with masterly economy. In a series of pungent constructs his sensibility sums up their inexorable limitations: they *All* (the capitalization should be noted) "have thirty-one." The poet's sensibility communicates a feeling to the sensibility of the reader so that the sensibility of both, with reference to their previous but independent sensibilities, is fused into that momentary communion of sensibility which is the final sensibility that poetry can give both to the sensibility of the poet and the sensibility of the reader. The texture and structure of the poem have erupted into a major reaction. The ambiguity of equilibrium is achieved.

7.

Against these two groups of spatial, temporal and numerical measurements—one consisting of four months, the other of seven—the tragic individual, the sole exception, "February," is dramatically placed. February is "alone," is

cut off from communion with his fellows. The tragic note
is struck the moment "February" is mentioned. For the
initial sound of the word "excepting" is "X," and as that
sound strikes the sensibility of the reader's ear a number
of associations subconsciously accumulate. We think of the
spot, the murderous and lonely spot, which "X" has so
frequently marked; we remember the examinations of our
childhood where the wrong answers were implacably sig-
naled with "X"; we think of ex-kings and exile, of lonely
crossroads and executions, of the inexorable anonymity of
those who cannot sign their names. . . .

8.

And yet the poet gives us one ray of hope, though it
eventually proves to be illusory. The lonely "February"
(notice how the "alone" in line four is echoed by the "only"
in line five), the solitary and maladjusted individual who
is obviously the hero and crucial figure of the poem, is not
condemned to the routine which his fellows, in their different ways, must forever obey. Like Hamlet, he has a capacity for change. He is a symbol of individualism, and the
rhythm of the lines which are devoted to him signalizes a
gayety, however desperate, which immediately wins our
sympathy and reverberates profoundly in our sensibility.

9.

But (and this is the illusion to which I have previously
referred) in spite of all his variety, his capacity for change,
"February" cannot quite accomplish (and in this his tragedy
consists) the *quantitative* value of the society in which circumstances have put him. No matter how often he may
alternate from twenty-eight to twenty-nine (the poet, with
his exquisite sensibility, does not actually *mention* those
humiliating numbers), he can never achieve the bourgeois, if
anonymous, security of "thirty-one," nor equal the more

modest and aristocratic assurance of "thirty." Decade after
decade, century after century, millennium after millennium, he is eternally frustrated. The only symbol of change
in a changeless society, he is continually beaten down. Once
every four years he tries to rise, to achieve the high, if delu-
sive, level of his dreams. But he fails. He is always one day
short, and the three years before the recurrence of his next
effort are a sad interval in which the remembrance of previous disappointment melts into the futility of hope, only
to sink back once more into the frustration of despair. Like
Tantalus he is forever stretched upon a wheel.

10.

So far I have been concerned chiefly with the dynamic
analysis of the poem. Further study should reveal the *synthesis* which can be made on the basis of the analysis which
my thesis has tentatively attempted to bring to an emphasis.
This, perhaps, the reader with a proper sensibility can achieve
for himself.

—Theodore Spencer

The Greatest English Lyric?— A New Reading of Joe E. Skilmer's "Therese"

 Genuine revolutions in literary taste and theory occur on an average only once every seven generations; therefore it is a source of satisfaction to have myself piloted what may be the most shattering reappraisal in our literature. I am referring—as the world of letters now knows well—to the discovery (made about the time that flying saucers began to be widely observed here and abroad) of that core of inner *is*-ness in the poetry of the long misread, long underrated Joburt Eggson Skilmer, or Joe E. Skilmer as he himself signed his poems. Slighted by serious readers for what seemed the facility of his technique and the pious banality of his thought—especially as shown in the poem known as "Trees"—Skilmer was in reality the perpetrator of an existentialist hoax on a public that prided itself on knowing what was genuine.

For years, many of us had been dissatisfied with the reading generally accorded this remarkable poem—the kind of official reading that provoked academic guffaws in a thousand classrooms. "There is more here than meets thee, eye," I would murmur to myself, teased by a host of ambiguities, of velleities that never quite came clear. It was a question of tone. Perhaps my first breakthrough came when I heard

Professor Wrugson O. Muttson reading a line from Pound's "The River-Merchant's Wife: A Letter":

> At fourteen I married my Lord you.

Muttson read the line as if it expressed wifely devotion. But it was obvious to me, as to any especially sensitive reader, that Pound intended the line to be heavily ironic, and that the "tone" might better be represented by something like

> At fourteen I married (my Lord!) *you?*

My trouble had been that I was ventriloquizing, putting my own voice into the poem, instead of letting it *read itself to me.* Do not read poems—this became my principle—be read to by them. This approach led to a number of discoveries, of which possibly the most earth-shaking was my article proving that Hamlet's famous soliloquy is not about suicide at all but about his meteorological and alchemical experiments with a number of test tubes (the "retorts" he is famous for), of which the tube lettered "E" seemed the most promising if the most vexatious:

> Tube "E" or not tube "E"—that is the quest, chum.
> Weather? 'Tis no blur in the mind . . .

But this reading, now officially adopted in the best textual editions, is too well known to need further quotation. I have also found my method of "deep reading" fruitful in the perusal of several thousand lines of *Paradise Lost,* and I suspect that our whole literature will have to be reread in the light of it. However: it was on the basis of this strict principle that I returned to Skilmer's great love poem to Therese Murk of Peoria. Called simply "Therese," or "T'rese," it had too long been thought of as having something to do with "trees"! The misconception arose from Skilmer's supreme irony; he had all too successfully "achieved an overlay," as he liked to say when speaking of the technique of poetry. That is, by a triumph of art he had given a shallow surface glaze, a pretty spindrift, to the profound abysses of the poem—a glaze so *trompe-l'oeil* that many were never able to see beneath it. What the public had been doing was reading only the "overlay" instead of what he called the "substruct," and what they settled for was something miserably like this:

> I think that I shall never see
> A poem lovely as a tree.
>
> A tree whose hungry mouth is pressed
> †Upon† the earth's sweet flowing breast.
>
> Upon whose bosom snow has lain,
> †And† intimately lives with rain.
>
> A tree that looks †at† God all day,
> And lifts her leafy arms to pray.
>
> A tree that may in summer wear
> A nest of robins in her hair.
>
> Poems are made by fools like me,
> But only God can make a tree.

Sheer banality! (And how far short of Skilmer's own noble definition of a poem as a "shimmering spitball flung into the great catcher's-mitt of eternity.") But the poem's *innerness,* which my researches have arrived at, is another thing entirely. What I mean to do here is demonstrate the "substruct," unit by unit, explicating where I can, though it is doubtful that any reader, or group of readers, will ever arrive at an adequate notion of the riches hidden in this most wonderful of poems.

1.

> *I* think? That I shall never, see!
> Up, owe 'em love. Leah's a tree.

Probably not since John Donne's "For Godsake hold your tongue, and let me love" has a poem opened with such explosive élan. "*I* think?" he rages; and in that fury is a ringing refusal to see life merely in terms of the "cogitations" that have amazed lesser poets. Here the whole Eliotic tradition of intellectualized verse is swept cleanly away forever —an achievement the more remarkable inasmuch as that tradition had not yet come into being. But few poets have had antennae so sensitive, been so unfailing a Tiresias (Therese? Ah yes!) in divining the yet-to-come. Crass indeed is the reader who fails to sense, in the proemial words, the poet's curling lip,[1] or who fails to note the hoot of scorn in the derisive "see" that concludes the line with a vulgarity ah how *voulu*! Almost blatant, this effect; and yet, beneath the brassy fanfare, what delicate counterpoint of grammatical woodwinds in the antiphony of declarative mood to interrogative, an antiphony that becomes harangue when we feel it in terms of the inner dialogue, the colloquy of a soul tormented by an age when all values have turned moot. Yet, as always in Skilmer, violence tempered with amenity: instead of the scowling "will" of resolution, only the disclaiming modesty of that simple "shall."

The second line, opening with courage and defiance, can but deepen the stated theme. "Up!" (cf. the Italian "Su! coraggio!") as the poet, confronting the inenarrable chaos of his world, lifts himself from that slough of despond by the Muses' very bootstrap. Don't *give* love away, he exhorts himself; don't wanton away so rare a substance on the all and sundry. *Owe* them love; do not pay when payment is despised. How much terser these moving words than such romantic maundering as

> When I was one-and-twenty
> I heard a wise man say,
> "Give crowns and pounds and guineas
> But not your heart away . . ."

But—oh marvel of art—again the tight-lipped acerbity is softened by one of the loveliest transitions in all poetry.

---

[1] Crudd P. Crass, "Joe E. Skilmer's Uncurling Lip," *LBJ*, lx, 167–761.

After the corrosive cynicism of the opening, the gentle evocation of Biblical womanhood fuses, as in Dante, with the mythology of the ancient world, in a line that sums up the fugacity of all things mortal. "Leah's a tree" indeed; Leah has *become* a tree, has escaped from the aggressor's pursuit, from the weary wheel of being. When Skilmer says "Leah" he is of course thinking of Daphne—the names have three letters (if no more) in common; our poet works by preference in that hallowed *three,* perhaps more meaningfully here than elsewhere, since in his sturdy American dialect *Therese* and *threes* would have been pronounced alike. It is no accident that the number of lines in the poem (12) is easily divisible by three, with none left over. Characteristic too of Skilmer's esemplastic knack is this grafting of image onto image; it is wholly natural that in thinking of the Ovidian Daphne he should conceive of her *a lo divino*—see her not as some mincing pagan, but aureate in the scriptural halo that Dante too looped like lassoes of tinsel round her.

2.

A tree—who's hung? Greymouth is pressed
Upon the earth-Swede, Flo Ingbrest.

A tree is indeed a tree, embodies as nothing else the very essence of the arboreal. An image of the world's green beauty— but no less an emblem of its horror. Skilmer's panoramic imagination sees the tree as a death-image, a very gallows with its dismal fruit. Painstaking Dantists ("In our age," the poet dourly quipped, "there are no painless Dantists") may well see here the influence of Dante's Wood of the Suicides.

We have learned little about Flo Ingbrest—Florence C. Ingbrest of 1222 Stitt St., Des Moines. Her very address is known only because it was found tattooed on the left hip of a sailor washed ashore at Tampa after the great hurricane of '23. It is clear that Miss Ingbrest meant much to the poet, who saw in this simple Swedish girl a power participating so fully in the chthonic matriarchal atavism of the dark earth itself that he calls her simply his "earth-Swede." Her earthy affections, however, were soon alienated by the vague and sinister figure the poet calls Greymouth, a misty shape ominous as any of the ghosts that slink nameless through the early Eliot. Though much research has been done on the unknown Greymouth, little has been ascertained. Dr. Woggs Clurth, basing his argument soundly on the morpheme "rey" in Greymouth, has proposed that he was really Watson King of Canton, the affable rapist; Dr. Phemister Slurk, dispensing with what he derides as "evidence," has suggested that he represents Warren G. Harding, an Ohio politico of the '20's. Cavillings all: Greymouth, whosoever he may have "been" in the world we think of as real, now, through Skilmer's artistry, exists forever in the purlieus of the Muse—slinking, loose-lipped, drivelling, livid with his nameless vice.

3.

> Upon whose boozin's (no!) *has* lain
> Anne D'Intagh Mittley—lives wi' Thrane.

In the third stanza, sometimes insensitively printed as the fifth, the tragedy grows blacker yet. After Florence C. Ingbrest and a handful of casual flames, the poet sought solace with the Mittley sisters of Boston. Researchers have shown that there were two: Daisy (or "Diz") Mittley, and her much younger sister Anne D'Intagh. It was the younger the poet loved, but again the romance was blighted by a conniving interloper, this time the wealthy Thaddeus Thrane of Glasgow, whose nationality is slyly derided in the dialectal "wi" for "with." The butt of frequent barbs in the Skilmer corpus, he is here dismissed with a contemptuous phrase. Though his beloved Anne lived "wi' " Thrane at the time the poem was written, Skilmer seems less troubled by this passing infidelity than by her amour with Greymouth—for Greymouth is the true antecedent of "whose." We now learn that he was a heavy drinker—and immediately the mysterious

soubriquet is clear. Extensive research has established that
gris is the common French word for *grey*. But *gris* also
means *drunk*. Greymouth then is unmasked as Drunk Mouth.
Indeed, so great a guzzler was Greymouth that the loyal
Miss Mittley was said, by a witty metonomy (or synecdoche)[2]
to have lain not on his bosom but (with a pun that anticipates Joyce by several weeks) on his "boozin's." One almost
hesitates to mention that "bosoms" too has its questionable
advocates.[3] Be that as it may, one wonders if in all literature the tragedy of four lives has been so harrowingly
adumbrated? All one can conjure up for comparison is
Dante's

Siena me fè; disfecemi Maremma.

But Dante, with his five and a half words for one life,
is long-winded compared with Skilmer, who averages a mere
three words per head, or even less, if one counts the "wi'"
as fractional diction. In this grisly aperçu, so true of all
humanity, the resources of typography too are put to unexampled use, with the two-letter "no" followed by an
exclamation mark that is like a spine straight with moral
indignation, and enclosed in the semicircularity of paren-
theses, like lips rounded in incredulous refusal. But the "no"
is uncompromisingly jostled by the assertive *has,* with its
harsh aspirate, distorted from honest Roman type into
italics, set askew from the vertical: even the letters, means
the poet, have *lost their aplomb* before the moral horror.
(A textual note: there are those, and their name is legion,[4]
who read "Hugh Inta Mittley" in the second line. But
nothing in Skilmer's emotional history gives countenance to
a suppositious passion for Anne's little brother Hugh, then
three years and some months old.)

[2] Clementine P. Pugh, "Joe E. Skilmer: Metonomy Si Synecdoche No!" *EETX,* cxl, 930–954.

[3] Louis P. ("Lew") Gubrious, "Greymouth:

Effeminate Lecher," *PMLX,* clv, 10–656.

[4] Lemuel P. and Lizzie X. Legion, "Who's Hugh in American Letters," *ACDC,* xi, 1066–1492.

4.

A tree that *looks* it!—Gawd! Auld, eh?
And Liffs hurl eavey alms, *tout prêts.*

And so it goes. The world-weariness, the melancholy, Skilmer in the depths of his Hamlet mood, or what he himself ruefully called, in the bad German he had learned from "certain ladies" in Milwaukee, "meines Hamletische Gesauerpusskeit." Does even Hamlet, whom so many have called the "Danish Skilmer," have a line so weary, stale, flat, and unprofitable as "A tree that *looks* it"?—in which the poet accepts the humble monotony of things as they are in their weary *haecceitas,* the sad fact that they are only what they are and so fully *look* what they are, instead of embodying the splendor of their Platonic archetypes. "The interminable pyramical napkin," broods E. E. Cummings—but how sesquipedalian this in comparison with Skilmer's demotic oomph. And from time immemorial this nauseating sameness—old indeed, and more than old. Probably there is no more plangent understatement in the language than Skilmer's simple but despairing "auld." For the poet, unable to tear his ravaged heart from thoughts of Thrane, glumly Scotticizes: "Auld, eh?" he spits out, thereby more keenly identifying Thrane with all he most distrusts in reality. Cosmic gloom induces wide-ranging speculations: the bard's restless mind hovers around the anthropology he loved so deeply, and from what sad strata of the past he must have disinterred his pregnant and touching lines about the Liffs. A Liff, as we know now, is the baseborn son of a Riff father and a Lett mother.* But even a Liff, born who knows where in semi-savagery, may hurl the alms of charity (as the miserly Thrane never did), alms that shelter us like eaves from the

*So Professor Nims alleges. There are others who take a less simplistic view. "Liff," as every schoolboy knows, is the way Dubliners refer to the River Liffey, whose waves are here in reference, since one casts alms, or bread, upon the waters. It would seem that Skilmer is alluding to the future *Finnegan's Wake* (Anna Livia Plurabelle) which was to be so profoundly influenced by "Therese." *Editor.*

cold and rook-delighting heaven, alms that are always ready, *tout prêts,* to relieve us. In his polyglot technique, Skilmer, as so often, again anticipates the practice of Ezra Pound, his foremost epigone: he uses the French words to imply that even the barbarous Liffs have achieved a measure of urbanity, as compared with certain uncivilized Scots he could mention. The touch of Gallic vivacity brightens, but all too briefly, the poem's Stygian verge. (Again, a textual note: some read "A tree that looks *two,*" and explain it as referring to the illusory nature of perceived reality. Rubbish![5])

5.

A tree . . . that Mayan summer! 'Ware
Honesta Robbins! Henna hair!

In explicating this *locus classicus* of modern poetry, it is necessary to bear in mind certain facts about the manuscripts—or "menu-scraps," as Skilmer himself wryly called them. Always a victim of poverty, the poet used to quill his sublimest ditties on the backs of labels laboriously soaked off the bottles of whiskey on which he shrewdly spent what little means the world afforded him. Thousands of these labels have survived, mute testimony to the trembling fingers that treasured them—each bearing only a few words of that great cornucopia of song he willed posterity. (There are also three labels from spaghetti cans, and one from a small can of succotash.) A study of some hundreds of manuscripts shows that Skilmer first wrote "A tree . . . that Aztec summer!"—a reference to the year he spent in Central America with an anthropological expedition. An idyllic year, possibly the happiest of his life, when his natural warmth and high spirits, so often thwarted by dingy circumstance, overflowed with an almost boyish ebullience. Arriving in early May, he had been married there three times by late June—and each time happily. Hence the little

[5] Wozlok DeTritus, "Rubbish-Schmub-
bish: the Ding-an-sich in Late-Middle
Skilmer," *RSVP,* ix, 51–52.

idyll about the Aztec summer, found on the manuscript
Old Overholt 202 and certain others. (The spaghetti labels
have little authority.) But the definitive reading is to be
found on *Heaven Hill 714:* not "Aztec" but "Mayan," a
word which Skilmer pronounced with the long *a* of *May.*
"A tree . . . that Mayan summer!"—and there it is forever,
the bright leaves bathed in a golden haze of old romance,
lost histories. An idyll, yes—but before long Skilmer's domestic
bliss was shattered. He was followed to Yucatan by Mrs.
Chloe P. Robbins of Ashtabula, a steamfitter's widow. With
her came her daughter, the 47-year-old Honesta Lou, whom
Skilmer called his "buxom nymph o' siren voice"—she was six
feet two, her flaring red hair vivid with purple highlights.
It is this vision of somewhat menacing loveliness that is
now evoked in lines that recall Coleridge's

> Beware, beware,
> His flashing eyes! his floating hair!

With deft economy, Skilmer laments the timelessness of
his plight by using the archaic " 'Ware" for "Beware."

6.

> Po' Em's our maid. 'Bye, fools! Like me,
> Butt only. Godkin may kertree!

Almost from the beginning, it was clear to a happy few
that what seemed "poem" was really "Po' Em," a poor
Southern girl named Emma or Emily. Her identity long
eluded researchers, until Dr. Cecily P. Wunkhead, basing
her argument largely on blood tests, litmus paper, and *Old
Crow 1066* (and rejecting the famous "succotash reading"
as spurious) proposed that the unknown Em was none
other than Emily Dickinson. To show that Emily is the
mouthpiece not only for New England but for all America
Skilmer resorts to an amazingly simple device: he gives
her a *southern* voice: probably not since Praxilla has the
ethos of inner dynamic been so functionally aligned with
dialectal specificity.

And why Emily Dickinson? Because she is the American Muse, ever at our side to lend a helping hand with torch on high—a servant, she, of servants of the laurel. Po' Em's our *maid,* and with our trust in her we can afford to dismiss the vulgar many, as Skilmer does with much the same testy arrogance that Yeats and Jonson flaunted. Whereas Jonson needed ten words or so in his

> Far from the wolves' dark jaw, and the black asses' hoof . . .

Skilmer does it in two burning words, "'Bye, fools!" But immediately compassion returns, and he remembers that the ordinary man, just as he, is only a butt for the slings and arrows of outrageous fortune. This might have set a-moping a less resilient bard, but Skilmer recovers, to conclude with a thundering diapason of *Jubel und Ruhm* such as not even Beethoven has ever equalled: the magnificent "Godkin may kertree!" Godkin: a little god, the least of the divinities in man, godkin *may*—but how the gala vowel, long *a,* implies lyric certainty in a word which, heard by the intellect alone, might seem to allow for doubt. *May* what? He may "kertree"! It is fitting that the pinnacle of Skilmer's sublimity should glitter in this final phrase of his greatest poem. And how like him to achieve sublimity by means so simple! Here he seizes from its lexical limbo the humble prefix *ker-,* as in *kerplunk, kerplop, kerflooie.* A prefix that only once before in English has assumed nobility, in J. F. Dudley-Andover's sublime translation of Dante's

> E caddi come corpo morto cade

as

> I plopped kerplunk, as corpses plop kerplunk.

Holding the precious *ker-* in the jeweler's forceps of his wit, Skilmer works it into a new thing entirely by fusing it with the unexpected "tree": to "kertree," to burst into flower, into foliage, nay, into very tree itself! One sees the creativity of the universe, the vital breath taking form in a great

efflorescence of green, a cosmic sneeze as if the whole sweet
growth of April and May, by some cinematic magic, were
effected in an instant.[6]
It is around this magical last line that scholarship itself
tends oftenest to kertree. "Godkin" in particular has stimu-
lated the finest hermeneutic acumen of our century to new
Everests of perception. Professor Fiedler has explored in
depth the profound viscerality of "gutkin." The Cambridge
School has constructed a breath-taking new theory of the
origin of tragedy on the reading "goat-kin." It is hardly
surprising that "incentive psychologists" make much of
"goadkin." Professor Fitts, citing γαδ- and χνων, finds a fish-
dog, or dogfish, allusion that unfortunately cannot be discussed in these pages. Nor can the suggestion of certain
Welshmen, who urge an early form of "gwiddcwyngh." Professor Rákóczi is more to the point in reminding us of what
careless readers might forget: "gyödzskin" is a medieval
South Hungarian gypsy cant word (though hardly the most
common) for a thickish wine made out of half-rotted arti-
chokes: what vistas open here! Only recently Nopançópi
Hópail has removed the whole question from the field of
linguistic speculation to that of biographical allusion by
proposing—how imaginatively!—that "godkin" is "Godkin":
E. L. Godkin (1831–1902), who came to America from Ireland
when twenty-five, founded *The Nation,* and was a disciple
of the Bentham-Mill-Grote school of philosophy.
On the whole subject, however, no one commands more
respect than Professor Fredson Bowers, whose monumental
fifty-volume edition of Skilmer, *The Fourteen Poems and
Certain Fragments,* is promised for 1970 by the Southeastern
Arkansas Junior Teachers' College Press. As early as 1962
Professor Bowers wrote: "I wonder if you have thoroughly
considered the evidence of *Old Crow 16*? In this version,
possibly a trial, 'May' is capitalized and must therefore be

---

[6] Skilmer's neologism has itself kertreen. One example out of many: Nancy Hale, one of Skilmer's most sensitive readers, has written, "The flowering of New England, that literary outpouring, kertreed everywhere . . ." *New England Discovery* (Coward-McCann, 1963), p. 353.

taken as the month.[7] If this is so, the possibility obtains
that the godkin referred to is the month of May, and hence
we can explain the diminutive. After all, in the month of
vernal growth there is something godlike in the creative
surge of the sap and the burgeoning of the chlorophyll.
However, the syntax is then in question. There is perhaps no
need to associate 'godkin May' with the 'butt,' even though
a month that pretends to be a little god might be a butt
for something. I think on the whole we are to take 'godkin
May's' activities with approval, not with disapproval. If so,
then I suggest that Skilmer, overcome with the wonder of
vegetable love and the rites of spring, finds that normal
syntax deserts him and is reduced to two paired but mutually
discrete exclamations. 'Godkin May!' or: Oh the wonder of
it all! And then that exclamation that sums up the plosive
force of May, 'Kertree!' "

This is brilliantly reasoned and would seem to be the last
word on the subject—but Professor Bowers had not yet
done with it. A few years later he decided that the line had
further subtleties, which he explained, in bibliographical
terms, as follows: "It could be read as a series of ejaculations,
rising to a climax. The lack of punctuation appropriate for
this reading is of course nothing unusual with Skilmer. That
is: only Godkin—the one God—He only. Then, in remembered
ecstasy of that Mexican spring, May [and here Professor
Bowers shows his grasp of contemporary allusion] just
busting out all over, like the bursting sap, the springing
leaf, in the ultimate mystical union with Nature, kertree!
Thus exclamation points should be placed after each unit.
I suggest these are at least alternate readings."

But perhaps these are matters beyond the power of man
to determine. However it may be, Godkin may indeed
kertree—but it takes a poet of supreme insight to perceive
this, a poet able to wrest language from dead strata of the

---

[7] Professor Bowers has established elsewhere the fact that Skilmer refused to accept "May" as a girl's name. "You might as well say 'June' is a girl's name," the poet would guffaw. Cf. F. Bowers, "Skilmer and the Non-Nomenclature of Womenfolk," QED, lx, 7-9.

past and kerplunk it living in the midst of men. But explication is no substitute for the poem. Here, for the first time presented in its ur-textual splendor, is what many* would consider the greatest lyric poem of our literature:

THERESE

By Joe E. Skilmer

I think? That I shall never, see!
Up, owe 'em love. Leah's a tree.

A tree—who's hung? Greymouth is pressed
Upon the earth-Swede, Flo Ingbrest.

Upon whose boozin's (no!) *has* lain
Anne D'Intagh Mittley—lives wi' Thrane.

A tree that *looks* it!—Gawd! Auld, eh?
And Liffs hurl eavey alms, *tout prêts*.

A tree . . . that Mayan summer! 'Ware
Honesta Robbins! Henna hair!

Po' Em's our maid. 'Bye, fools! Like me,
Butt only. Godkin may kertree!

---

*Does this include Professor Ian Watt?
Editor.

SUPPLEMENTARY DOCUMENTS

SONNET 129

These sad fragments, so like the papyri of Sappho preserved in the hot dry sands of Oxyrrhynchus (in Egypt), were recovered, tattered and charred, from a box of hot dry sand at Luxor (in South Dakota), which had been kept near a woodstove in the railroad station for the use of brakemen. Typed out by Skilmer, the poem is indubitably his, since it bears in his own handwriting the inscription "My fav[o]rite poem." A writer as careful with words as our poet would hardly write "my" if he meant the exact opposite: "someone else's." Even these poor scraps were preserved only by a lucky chance. Run through a meatgrinder (luckily coarse) with the daily hamburger, the mélange was promptly bolted by a small coonhound named Harold, whose stomach as promptly rejected

the unwonted fare, depositing it unceremoniously on the warm sand
by the stove, where the pieces were buried from sight as the sands
shifted in drafts from the opening door. Fortunately, the very next
day a head-on collision killed sixty-six passengers and tore up a
half mile of track. The spur line was not thought worth repair-
ing; the station was closed, and only an occasional vagrant would
stoke up the stove that kept warm the fostering sand. The papyroids
are somewhat stained by tobacco juice.

Discovered by an amateur thrill-seeker in 1953, they were en-
trusted to Professor Koch-Schurr for restoration. Schooled in the
methods of M. M. Edmonds (who from a ten-word fragment of
Sappho was unfailingly able to reconstruct the lost original, many
times as long), Professor Koch-Schurr set to work. He immediately perceived that the key lay in such words as "expense,"
"trust,"—and, for the poet's attitude—"blame." The poem, he concluded, was therefore an attack on an economic system. "Spirit[s],"
in Skilmer's vocabulary, almost surely meant the kind of spirits
he knew best. Working from this slim basis of certainty, Professor
Koch-Schurr succeeded in restoring the poem to what most scholars
will agree is essentially what Skilmer wrote. Here, then, given for
the first time to a waiting world, is one of the bard's most significant masterpieces *exactly* as he may have written it—a very
fundament of the mighty corpus!

SONNET 129

The expense of spirits is a crying shame!
Is lust for lucre (money, man!). 'Twould bust
'Is personal nest-egg was 'e Croesus!—blame
Savings & Loans that back the liquor trust.
Enjoyed no sox, sax, sex, soup, soap or sup?
Past reach of average man, the price-tag soar;
Parade on high like bloomy larks. Up up
On purple-fringèd wing, red debits roar.

Ma[d in pursuit and in possession so,]*
Hairy as haystacks, and in quest of grails?
Stand on the roof and proposition Flo?
(What have the little lambs behind: heads? tails?)
All this the worried man can murmur: sell
To shun going broke. Being broke's like heaven? Like hell.

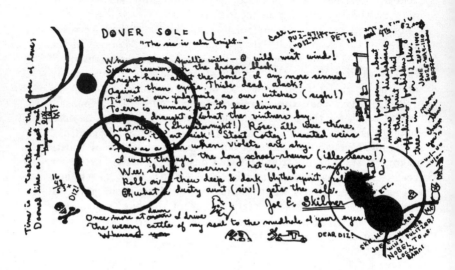

CUTTY SARK 711 (*Dover Sole*)

Cutty Sark 711 (fondly called "The Emperor Manuscript") gives us the only known "fair copy" of a Skilmer poem. This precious document, the glory of the British Museum, bears some of the characteristic watermarks found on many of the poet's papers: they are circular and about four centimeters across (roughly the size of a standard "jigger" or "shot glass"). Many things about this touching relic, so rich in humanity, suggest that something fierier than mere quill of mortal has been here set down. It is little wonder that a leading critic of Belleville (Illinois) has called it "a very Sinai of the spirit."

---

*"Here my inspiration forsook me," laments Professor Koch-Schurr, "yielding only a line flat, jejune, unpoetic— quite without the afflatus of the Sweet Swan of just outside Peoria."

The text of *Dover Sole* has been extensively studied. Apparently one of the poet's earliest works, it shows a thorough familiarity with the achievements of English poetry up to, and perhaps beyond, his time. Academic critics, insensitive to the workings of inspiration and true creativity, have dismissed it as "derivative" and even "sheer pastiche"!

Almost heartbreaking in their ruined beauty are Skilmer's jottings around the margin—mere luminous inklings of a dawn no sooner bloomed than blasted. Of the haunting "Time is a toadstool on the nose of love," I. A. Leavis-Beehynde has written, "If this is not the finest metaphor in recent European literature, I just don't know what." And surely no poet has ever so summed up the spirit of the American desert, its unpeopled multi-scorpioned mirage-bemused vastitudes, the lone charisma of its sandy avatars, as has our poet in his

> Once more at dawn I drive
> The weary cattle of my soul to the mudhole of your eyes.

The numerals and occult code-names on "The Emperor" would seem to be part of a system the secretive poet devised to record his rhythmical inventions. Instead of just saying *ta-dum, da-dum*.

—John Frederick Nims

Eliot Among the Nightingales: Fair and Foul

". . . c'est pour les oiseaux."—*Baudelaire.*
"I am . . . befouled."—*The Family Reunion.*
"Drip drop drip drop drop drop drop."—*The Waste Land.*

Although critical and analytical examinations of the poetry of T. S. Eliot abound in such numbers that further exegesis and commentary would seem to be, to say the least, supererogatory, a recent reading of the *oeuvre* has revealed to me a hitherto undiscussed aspect of the poet's thought and imagery. Eliot's principal symbols are, of course, familiar to the man in the street, thanks to the many detailed studies of his metaphor. The merest novice in literature knows the significance of Eliot's use of the wheel, the rose garden, the rock, water, hair, and hyacinths, to name only a few of the recurrent symbols. But an exceptionally revealing insight into the poet's mind and art may be had through a consideration of another cluster of objects which function symbolically in his work—a strand of imagery both complex and subtle, which, unaccountably, has never yet been the subject of close examination.

We may begin by noting some significant terminology in an important exchange between Agatha and Harry, in *The Family Reunion.* Describing a crucial experience from her past, Agatha associates it most clearly with a particular observed detail: "And then a black raven flew over." Harry, attuned to his aunt's psychic wave-length, responds intuitively, and meaningfully refers to a similar experience as

"the awful evacuation." And a few moments later he speaks
of his present predicament in the following relevant phrase:
"I am still befouled." Describing elsewhere the nature of this
feeling, in somewhat greater detail, he says:

> . . . the slow stain sinks deeper through the skin
> Tainting the flesh and discolouring the bone—
> . . . it is unspeakable.

And a further detail:

> You do not know
> The noxious smell traceable in the drains.

This feeling is also developed several times in *Murder in
the Cathedral,* in the choruses spoken by the women of
Canterbury:

> . . . now a new terror has soiled us,
> Which none can avert, none can avoid,
> Flowing under our feet and over the sky.

And again:

> We are soiled by a filth that we cannot clean . . .
> It is not we alone, it is not the house, it is not the city
>   that is defiled,
> But the world that is wholly foul.
> Clear the air! clean the sky! wash the wind!

The source of this defilement is referred to in terms which
confirm Agatha's symbol:

> The Lords of Hell are here.
> They . . . swing and wing through the dark air.

Furthermore,

> . . . through the dark air
> Falls the stifling scent . . .;
> The forms take shape in the dark air.

The various forms which "take shape in the dark air" are
remarkably numerous throughout the body of Eliot's work;
a few of the more interesting ones will be enumerated below. It is relevant to note first, however, that they are not
motiveless, nor is their behavior purely instinctive:

> . . . the . . . hawk
> Will only soar and hover, circling lower,
> Waiting excuse, pretence, opportunity.
> *(Murder in the Cathedral)*

And it will be recalled that the bird which flits through
"Burnt Norton" is full of imperatives (perhaps to his companions): "Quick, said the bird, find them, find them"; and
also "Go, go, go, said the bird."

The somewhat nervous speaker in "A Cooking Egg" asks
the apprehensive question, "Where are the eagles?" This
is answered, if obliquely, by the pained exclamation of the
spectator of the parade in "Triumphal March," who says,
"And so many eagles!" and later, as if in desperation (note
the shift): "But how many eagles!" However, "The Eagle
[which] soars in the summit of Heaven" (*The Rock,* Chorus
I) is not the only bird inhabiting Eliot's aviary. The smallest
are "The small creatures [which] chirp thinly through the
dust" in "Difficulties of a Statesman." "Gerontion" finds
a gull sailing against the wind, and "Ash Wednesday" exhibits
a "dove descending [which] breaks the air," and "The cry
of quail and whirling plover," as well as "seaward flying/Un-
broken wings."[1]

The images of bird life are frequently found in conjunction with images of water, naturally enough. In "Ash Wednesday," for example, "the fountain sprang up and the bird
sang down." The first section of "Burnt Norton" describes
the effects capable of being wrought by a bird (the same one
which urges his fellows to "Go, go, go"):

---

[1] The title of *The Cocktail Party,* needless
to say, includes another reference to a
bird of a sort.

> Dry the pool, dry concrete . . .
> And the pool was filled with water . . .

Phlebas the Phoenician, a fortnight drowned, "forgot the
cry of gulls"; himself a part of the water now, he is no
longer pained to worry like the others: "What is that sound
high in the air?"

The "sound high in the air" is represented variously by
Eliot. In "The Waste Land," we find the sounds created
as "Twit, twit," "Tereu," "Co co rico," and "Jug, jug."[2]
But the most explicit of all these is the sound of the hermit-
thrush, which goes quite simply, "Drip drop drip drop drop
drop drop." The poet's attitude toward all this is that of
despairing acceptance. Thus, in "New Hampshire," he ex-
claims, apparently to bird-dom in general:

> Black wing, brown wing, hover over;
> . . . .
> Cover me over . . .

As the result of this attitude, the poet concludes (in "Lines
to a Persian Cat") that "Beneath the trees there is no ease,"
for the quite evident reason that this is where "The songsters
of the air repair." This same distrust of trees is echoed in
two poems of the fragmentary *Coriolan*. In "Triumphal
March," the "palmtree at noon" is inextricably associated
with the symbol of "running water"; in "Difficulties of a
Statesman," the emotion is so intense that the protagonist
finds himself speaking in broken phrases:

> O hidden under the . . . Hidden under the . . .
> Where the dove's foot rested and locked for a moment,
> . . . under the upper branches of noon's widest tree.

Eliot mocks those who are able to be truly at ease under a
tree, by parodying their unquestioning acceptance. In the
"Fragment of an Agon" from *Sweeney Agonistes,* the jazz
lyric satirizes the failure or the renunciation of discrimination.

---

[2] Incidentally, the "Jug, jug" reference,
while perhaps adequately explained by
Edmund Wilson, may have another meaning, particularly when taken in conjunction with the exclamation in Part V—"O
swallow swallow." I do not think that
this collocation has ever been pointed
out before.

> Tell me in what part of the wood
> Do you want to flirt with me?
> Under the breadfruit, banyan, palmleaf
> Or under the bamboo tree?
> Any old tree will do for me
> Any old wood is just as good . . .

Of all the various winged forms which wreak their vengeance from the air, however, none is more frightful than the eponymous beast in "The Hippopotamus." It will be recalled that, toward the end of the poem,

> The 'potamus takes wings
> Ascending from the damp savannas

The terrifying possibilities inherent in this transmogrification are realized in Harry's words from *The Family Reunion,* as he refers with horror to "The unexpected crash of the iron cataract."[3]

It is only thus when we examine Eliot's concept of birds ("The Lords of Hell") as embodiments of (literally) "unearthly" evil that we are able to account for a facet of his career which other critics have resolutely avoided, tacitly ignored, or politely assumed to be irrelevant. This is, of course, his role as the creator of the "Book of Practical Cats." These poems, which have not as yet been given the critical examination they so richly deserve, are clearly not incidental to his main development, but are part of it. This is not the place to undertake an extended discussion of the poems,[4] but it is certainly not amiss to point out that the natural enemies of birds are—cats. Nor should the significant adjective be overlooked. These are not idle house pets but active and energetic creatures; they are "practical" in the sense in which Lavinia, in *The Cocktail Party,* uses the word. Reject-

[3] The women of Canterbury may also be referring to this vision when, in enumerating the possibilities of Death, they chant of "the sudden shock upon the skull."

[4] An analysis demonstrating that the poems are an intricately-constructed symbolic structure dealing with the theme of Original Sin (and incidentally tracing the influences of Kierkegaard, Rilke, Dante, Edgar Wallace, and Massinger) is in the process of preparation by the author.

ing the ability to fill out an income-tax blank as evidence
of practicality, she says, "When I say practical, I mean
practical in the things that really matter." The alert reader
of Eliot is, of course, aware (1) that the Chamberlayne
household has no bird as pet; and (2) that Lavinia reveals
herself as capable of being exceptionally "catty." In the
final act, the reconciliation is partly due to Edward's
recognition of his wife's quality. "You have a very practical
mind," he tells her then.

* * *

"Suffering is action," Eliot has written. But some action
may be taken to prevent suffering—this is the implication of
another major strand of imagery which must be seen in
its proper relationship to the symbols of the birds. There
are two modes of response to the existence of implacable
evil from above. Harry Monchensey's decision to go into
the desert, like that of Celia Coplestone, represents one
way of outwitting the birds (there are no trees in the desert).
The other way is to adopt some kind of covering, some
defense, which may be either a hood, mantle, cap ("cape"),
or hat. This second mode of response may be defined as the
principle of protective coveration. It is clearly Eliot's intention to contrast those who adopt such a principle with
those who do not. "Lines for Cuscuscaraway and Mirza
Murad Ali Beg" describes Mr. Eliot as possessing "a wopsical
hat"; the picture is satirical but not unfavorable. On the
other hand, the companion piece has a sharply malicious
tone; in "Lines to Ralph Hodgson Esqre." the significant
lines are

> He has 999 canaries
> And round his head finches and fairies . . .

This bird-lover is obviously a friend of the "Lords of Hell,"
whereas the "unpleasant" Mr. Eliot may be described as
wearing a fragment which he shores up against the ruins.
    "The Waste Land," it will be recalled, contains many

people who adopt this principle: "Who are these hooded
hordes?" asks the protagonist in amazement. And he notices
especially another figure:

> There is always another one . . .
> Gilding wrapt in a brown mantle, hooded . . .

(It is not irrelevant to note that we are meant to associate
this figure with the Journey to Emmaus.)

A detail bothersome to previous critics of "Sweeney Among
the Nightingales" may now be cleared up easily. The reason
for the peculiar attire worn by the lady who attempts Sweeney's seduction—a Spanish cape—should now be apparent,
especially when it is remembered that the scene takes place
in a neighborhood where nightingales abound; furthermore,
there is evidence in the poem that these particular nightingales have been at their "liquid siftings" for some time, a
habit which would necessitate one's wearing a large garment
for protection whenever venturing out.

Eliot uses the technique of "covering up" his meaning at
the same time that he is dealing with the subject of "cover-
ing-up," a source of rich ambiguity and ironic tension, as
well as fruitful paradox, in his poetry. Thus he is able to
operate simultaneously at the levels of concrete generalities
and general details. One instance of this practice is the
precise naming of hats (perhaps a sly parallel echo to "The
Naming of Cats") throughout his poems, while still manag-
ing to disguise what he is doing. Thus, upon close scrutiny
"The Waste Land" reveals three obvious names of hats. The
most obvious (and therefore the one which previous critics
have never been able to account for) is found in the exclamation of the protagonist at the end of "The Burial of the
Dead." His friend's name, of course, is—*Stetson*! In the
chorus of the Thames nymphs, the sails are depicted as
swinging to "*Lee*ward," and "past the Isle of Dogs" (which,
with but slight alteration, may read as *"Dobbs"*). In the
fourth section of "East Coker," there is a significant reference to "*Adam*'s curse." And finally, to conclude this
brief but I trust convincing demonstration of a recurrent

device in Eliot, there is his extremely subtle use of the repeated "KNOCK" at the conclusion of *Sweeney Agonistes:* a series of "knocks" (*Knox*).

The hats may be of various kinds: we recall the "silk hat of a Bradford millionaire" in "The Waste Land," the straw "headpiece" of "The Hollow Men," and Celia Coplestone's urgent "feelings" (her *felt* need). But regardless of type or make, the "cover" is a necessity. And so, fittingly, under "cover" of madness, at the conclusion of "The Waste Land," Eliot-Hieronymo[5] undertakes to pass on to his sensitive and understanding auditors the most profound truths granted him by his intelligence and poetic vision. You must take cover, he cries, and if you do—

Why then Ile fit you.

—*Charles Kaplan*

[5] I.e., "The Mad Hatter." Need one comment on the obvious influence of Lewis Carroll upon Eliot's entire poetic corpus?

"Invictus": A Regurgitation

INVICTUS

By William Ernest Henley

Out of the night that covers me,
  Black as the Pit from pole to pole,
I thank whatever gods may be
  For my unconquerable soul.

In the fell clutch of circumstance
  I have not winced or cried aloud.
Under the bludgeonings of chance
  My head is bloody, but unbowed.

Beyond this place of wrath and tears
  Looms but the Horror of the shade,
And yet the menace of the years
  Finds, and shall find, me unafraid.

It matters not how strait the gate,
  How charged with punishments the scroll,
I am the master of my fate:
  I am the captain of my soul.

ᖇ *Invictus* describes man's reaction to life, and gives the poet's conclusions in terms of self-reliance. Night, he tells us, is "black as the Pit," but since he does not qualify the word "Pit," he makes subtle use of at least four of the currently available ambiguities. What kind of "Pit"—peach, orchestra, William? We can eliminate William since he has two t's. But what of that kind of pit which we associate with a declivity? The reader, as the poet intends, assumes the latter.

The affective significance of the words, in Stanza One, "from pole to pole," is heightened by the intertwining of two nouns with two prepositions, both nouns ("pole") being the same. This use of the homonym is given both life and motion by the use of two different prepositions, "from," and "to," the "from" significantly preceding, rather than following, the "to."

Lines three and four of Stanza One are purely conative, and show an almost overeager emotive use of language. Again the poet employs ambiguities (this time three out of a possible seven) in speaking of "whatever gods may be," rather than employing specific terms such as Baal, Hermes, Gog, or Di Maggio.

The first stanzaic division leads us directly to Stanza Two which is based on the poet's fundamental acceptance of the doctrine of logical irrelevance, as evidenced in the first two lines. What is the "fell clutch"? What made the clutch fall? Did the clutch fall or did it slip? If the clutch slipped why did not the poet have it repaired? Has he been riding the clutch? Is there grease in his crankcase?

In Stanza Three the nonexistent plot enters the structure of the poem. Here the poet informs us that beyond a certain place, characterized by "wrath and tears," there is considerable shade. This creates tension since the poet has just come "out of the night that covers me." Despite this, he would still seek the shade were the shade not horrible. In fact, he refers to it as a "Horror" which does not fall gently, like other horrors, but "looms." This is a highly revealing example of the poet's mordant use of the double mood.

Up to this point the poet has suffered considerable discomfort. He has been submerged in pitch blackness. His clutch has slipped. Chance has bludgeoned him. His head is bloody and he has lost his bow tie. No sooner does he escape the Horror of the shade than the years menace him. Then he discovers that the scroll charges him with various punishments. (*Cf. Adam, Abou Ben*).

Here we come to the nexus of the poem, which may be found primarily in its nonexistent symbolic value. The poet is telling us that despite the buffeting of fate ("bludgeonings of chance"), he remains the "master" of his destiny, the "captain" of his soul, terms which unite both ancient and modern sailing patois. As both "master" and "captain," he guides his vessel, which is himself, through the night, the Pit, and the horror of the shade.

He might have avoided all this if he had repaired his clutch.

CHRONOLOGY OF "INVICTUS"

8:30 a.m.	Poet arises. (This is an assumption, yet it is given credence by a recent New Critics Survey, *Rising Hour of British Poets, 1775–1925*).
8:45 a.m.	Discovers that night covers him. Confused, since clock indicates it is morning.
8:47 a.m.	Gives thanks to whatever gods may be.
9:00 a.m.	Breakfast.
9:15 a.m.	Clutch slips.
10:46 a.m.	Neither winces nor cries aloud.
11:00 a.m.	Low tea.
11:15 a.m.	Ends period of neither wincing nor crying aloud.
1:48 p.m.	Chance arrives, bloodies poet's head.
4:15 p.m.	High tea.
5:41 p.m.	Poet places cold towel on bloodied head.
7:34 p.m.	Horror of the shade looms.
8:00 p.m.	Dinner.
11:17 p.m.	Poet unlatches gate.

11:39 p.m.	Poet reads scroll, calls lawyer.
11:45 p.m.	Poet sleeps.
8:30 a.m.	Poet arises (Cf. New Critics Survey, *Rising Hour of British Poets, 1775–1925*).
9:23 a.m.	Poet goes to Bureau of Licenses to apply for master's and captain's papers.
6 Months Later	Poet receives master's and captain's papers. Immediately commences to guide fate and soul.
11:00 a.m.	Low tea.

—Ira Wallach

The Ghost of Christmas Past: "Stopping by Woods on a Snowy Evening"

∾ Much ink has spilled on many pages in exegesis of this little poem. Actually, critical jottings have only obscured what has lain beneath critical noses all these years. To say that the poem means merely that a man stops one night to observe a snowfall, or that the poem contrasts the mundane desire for creature comfort with the sweep of aesthetic appreciation, or that it renders worldly responsibilities paramount, or that it reveals the speaker's latent death-wish is to miss the point rather badly. Lacking has been that mind simple enough to see what is *really* there.

The first line ("Whose woods these are I think I know") shows that the speaker has paused beside a woods of whose ownership he is fairly sure. So much for paraphrase. Uncertainty vanishes with the next two lines ("His house is in the village though;/He will not see me stopping here"). The speaker knows (a) where the owner's home is located, and (b) that the owner won't be out at the woods tonight. Two questions arise immediately: (a) how does the speaker know? and (b) how does the speaker know? As will be made manifest, only one answer exists to each question.

The subsequent two quatrains force more questions to pop up. On auditing the first two lines of the second quatrain

("My little horse must think it queer/To stop without a farmhouse near"), we must ask, "Why does the little 'horse' think oddly of the proceedings?" We must ask also if this *is*, as the speaker claims, the "darkest evening of the year." The calendar date of this occurrence (or lack of occurrence) by an unspecified patch of trees is essential to an apprehension of the poem's true meaning. In the third quatrain, we hear "harness bells" shaken. Is the auditory image really an allusion? Then there is the question of the "horse's" identity. Is this really Equus Caballus? This question links itself to that of the *driver's* identity and reiterates the problem of the animal's untoward attitude toward this evidently unscheduled stop.

The questions have piled up unanswered as we reach the final quatrain and approach the ultimate series of poetic mysteries to be resolved. Clearly, all of the questions asked thus far (save possibly the one about the "horse's" identity) are ones which any normal reader, granted the training in close analysis proved by a survey course in English Literature during his sophomore year in college, might ask. After some extraneous imagery ("The woods are lovely, dark and deep" has either been established or is easily adduced from the dramatic situation), the final three lines hold out the key with which the poem's essence may be released. What, to ask two more questions, are the "promises" which the speaker must "keep," and why are the last two lines so redundant about the distance he must cover before he tumbles into bed? Obviously, the obligations are important, the distance great.

Now, if we swing back to one of the previous questions, the poem will begin to unravel. The "darkest evening of the year" in New England is December 21st, a date near that on which the western world celebrates Christmas. It may be that December 21st *is* the date of the poem, or (and with poets this seems more likely) that this is the closest the poet can come to Christmas without giving it all away. Who has "promises to keep" at or near this date, and who must traverse much territory to fulfill these promises? Yes, and who but St. Nick would know the location of *each* home? Only he would know who had "just settled down for a long winter's nap" (the poem's third line—"He will not see me stopping here"—is clearly a veiled allusion) and would not be out inspecting his acreage this night. The unusual phrase "fill up with snow," in the poem's fourth line, is a transfer of Santa's occupational preoccupation to the countryside; he is mulling the filling of countless stockings hung above countless fireplaces by countless careful children. "Harness bells," of course, alludes to "Sleighing Song," a popular Christmas tune of the time the poem was written, in which the refrain "Jingle Bells! Jingle Bells!" appears; thus again are we put on the Christmas track. The "little horse," like the date, is another attempt at poetic obfuscation. Although the "rein-reindeer" ambiguity has been eliminated from the poem's final version,[2] probably because too obvious, we may speculate that the animal is really a reindeer disguised as a horse by the poet's desire for obscurity, a desire which we must concede has been fulfilled up to now.

The animal is clearly concerned, like the faithful Rudolph— another possible allusion (post facto, hence unconscious)— lest his master fail to complete his mission. Seeing no farmhouse in the second quatrain, but pulling a load of presents, no wonder the little beast wonders! It takes him a full two quatrains to rouse his driver to remember all the empty stockings which hang ahead. And Santa does so reluctantly at that, poor soul, as he ponders the myriad farmhouses and villages which spread between him and his own "winter's nap." The modern St. Nick, lonely and overworked, tosses no "Happy Christmas to all and to all a good night!" into the precipitation. He merely shrugs his shoulders and resignedly plods away.

—Herbert R. Coursen, Jr.

[2] The original draft contained the following line: "That bid me give the reins a shake" (Stageberg-Anderson, *Poetry as Experience* [New York, 1952], p. 457).

Tales and Tailors
>>>>>>>>>>>>>>>>>>>>>>>>>>>>

The Secret of
"The Secret Sharer" Bared

⟲ One is finally forced to conclude of this story, as Miss Caroline Gordon did of Joyce's *Portrait,* that "this book has been misread by a whole generation."[1] Either the critics have outdone in reticence the late Victorian Conrad, or they have baffled themselves in searching out esoteric meanings and have failed to comprehend the *secret* of this story of two men at sea. For the technique of Conrad, obscuring while yet it shadows forth the meaning of the story, seems to have led all readers to treat "The Secret Sharer" variously as a story of murder, of first-command, of the Cain-Abel archetype,[2] whereas the story's meaning, once comprehended, is simple and straightforward. Surely it is time now to dispense with critical diffidence and say once for all that the true archetype of the story is the Hyacinthine and that its secret can consequently be summed up in one word: homosexuality.

Credit for recognizing that the story has an element of

[1] Caroline Gordon, "Some Readings and Misreadings," *Sewanee Review,* LXI (Summer 1953), 388.

[2] See, for example, Louis H. Leiter, "Echo Structures: Conrad's 'The Secret Sharer,'" reprinted in *Conrad's "Secret Sharer" and the Critics,* ed. Bruce Harkness (Wadsworth Publishing Company, 1962). All references to the story and many to the criticism are to this volume, hereafter cited as *Critics.*

sexual significance must go to Mr. Thomas Moser, who in his *Joseph Conrad: Achievement and Decline* commented on

> How often the various early heroes see their test, like the later lovers and voyeurs, through an open door! . . . The young captain cannot forget his double, sometimes asleep behind the bed-curtains, sometimes bolt upright behind the bathroom door. "The Secret Sharer" reminds us of the love stories in another way: it has two scenes in which at a critical moment a character drops an object in another's presence. The untested captain's lighted cigar . . . plops into the sea when he discovers Leggatt . . . at the bottom of the ladder. When they separate forever at the end of the story, Leggatt drops the captain's hat . . .[3]

Since Mr. Moser's analysis has other mythic purposes, it is quite understandable that he does not follow up this suggestion by analyzing the Hyacinthine motif of "The Secret Sharer," which is my purpose in this study.

Before interpreting the story in this new light, however, it seems necessary to marshal the evidence from the text that "The Secret Sharer" does in fact have as its subject, homosexuality. Once this evidence is adduced, brought to the surface as it were, the story can then be read in the light of its proper interpretation and seen as in fact what it is: the earliest mature interpretation of homosexual relations in English literature, fit to take its complementary place beside the work of Lawrence in analyzing the relations between a man and a woman. In fact, so astonishingly skillful is this work of early modern literature that its artistic achievement in the rendering of homoeroticism was not to be surpassed until the publication of Robin Maugham's Albertine archetype, *The Servant*.

With characteristic adroitness, then, Conrad has made explicit the homosexual nature of the relationship between

---

[3] Thomas Moser, *Joseph Conrad: Achievement and Decline* (Harvard University Press, 1957), pp. 129–130. In connection with Mr. Moser's observance that the Captain shares some traits with the voyeurs of Conrad's other stories, note that Leggatt says of himself as a nude swimmer, "I saw [the Captain's] head looking over. . . . I didn't mind being looked at. I—I liked it" (p. 15).

Leggatt and the Captain, while yet hiding it from his Edwardian readers and perhaps, for that matter, from his conscious self.[4] The evidence of the text is so striking that, once recognized as part of the imagery of the story, no other interpretation is possible, unless the story is taken as essentially meaningless. A close reading of the story makes this clear.

The first clue comes early—"My name's Leggatt" (p. 8). Despite the spelling Conrad could count on his readers' pronouncing, *Leg-it:* this revealing while seeming to hide is characteristic of the entire technique, for both words of course are slang (if not standard English) for the sexual organ and act.[5]

Beginning with this clue, all falls into place. Indeed, the very first word uttered by Leggatt is the monosyllable, "Cramp"—easily misheard at sea as *Camp* (p. 7). And as if not to let us miss the point of Leggatt's name, Conrad reemphasizes it a few pages later as the narrator helps Leggatt into his bedplace (which significantly has *drawers* underneath it): Leggatt needed the lift "I gave him by seizing his leg." This is surely an unnecessary operation for a man who "tumbled in" the bed, as one cannot "tumble into" a high bedstead, and Conrad is much too fine an artist to use words loosely.

[4] The reader should perhaps be reminded that Conrad was of slight and short stature, with highly polished and un-English aristocratic mannerisms. But to explore such possibilities any further is needless and misleading, since the solipsistic and unsophisticated genetic or intentional interpretation is quite beyond the necessities or purposes of the present study. This is true, even though as Mr. Albert Guerard says (*Critics*, p. 60) that "the myth of the night journey is unusually conscious in "The Secret Sharer.'" One might also discuss the relationship of Conrad to his character, Rita, and the duel with an American adventurer in *The Arrow* of Gold as well as the peculiar relationships of Heyst, Lena, and Jones in *Victory;* but these are tertiary arguments. Furthermore, as Miss Caroline Gordon says, "it is possible that the primal plot may operate in a work of art not only without the artist's conscious knowledge but almost against his will" (Gordon, p. 388).

[5] See Eric Partridge, *A Dictionary of Slang and Unconventional English.* As, "leg-lifter," a male fornicator; "leg-business," sexual intercourse. Partridge himself even hints at homosexuality: "it," the female, occ. the male, sexual organ.

Notice also the subtle technique whereby Conrad drives home the significance of this first physical contact of the men (a scene which is to be echoed later in the "wrestling" in the sail-locker). For immediately after, significantly, the Captain "was extremely tired, in a peculiarly intimate way. . ." (p. 16).

One is astounded by the ineptness of the critics' interpretation of the character of the narrator, for Conrad is explicit on the next page in discussing the attitude of the steward and crew toward the Captain. "I don't know whether the steward had told them that I was 'queer' only, or . . ." (p. 17). And again there are the curious repetitions (like the repetition of *leg*) in subsequent passages. The Captain had a "*queer* sense of whispering to" himself (p. 18, italics supplied). "But the *queerest* part . . ." (p. 23, italics supplied).

Notice also the mechanics of the movements in the famous L-shaped cabin. This Captain, though he had "no one to say nay to [him] within the whole circle of the horizon" (p. 17) goes through a long-drawn-out farce of hiding Leggatt from the crew even after Captain Archbold of the *Sephora* has left.[6] These always take a similar pattern: "Get into that bed" (p. 15). "We took up our position . . . leaning over my bedplace" (p. 24).[7] "I would smuggle him into my bedplace" (p. 26). "He stepped back and leaned against my bed" (p. 32).

All of this is surely revealing enough, although Conrad may have been unconscious of its revelation and asked

---

[6] Note that in real life, the Captain who received the murderer made no pretense of hiding him: such a thing is entirely unnecessary in the tradition of the sea of the 1880's. But of course the myths and even the rude jokes of the Navy and Mercantile Marine, though they may be a profanation of a dream, bear witness to homosexuality, at least latent, in maritime life. Query: What *is* the Captain's motive for hiding Leggatt from the officers and crew? Is it fear of sharing the sharer? (On the "original" of the story see the account by Basil Lubbock, reprinted in *Critics*). Further query: What are the rather mysterious reasons (p. 4) by which the Captain was free to take this new post? Could Conrad by hinting at "certain events of no particular significance, except to myself" which caused difficulties with previous owners and/or masters?

[7] For definitions, see Mr. John Sparrow on *Lady Chatterley* in *Encounter*, XVIII (February 1962), 35–43.

the Edwardian reader to believe that the purpose is only to "whisper together"—in a spacious cabin, in the middle of the night, when the two could sit on the couch in comfort behind a closed (and even locked) door! There can be no purpose, on the level of a maritime story of adventure, for repair to the bed to whisper; hence this reiterated detail, observable to any close reader of the text, must have some further significance. If the force of these passages has any purpose at all, that significance is clear.

In this—apparently—new context, a rereading of the story is especially revealing. In the very opening line the phallic symbol is introduced: "On my right hand there were lines of *fishing-stakes.* . . ."[8] Many other details assume a new meaning, deepening the texture of the story. Why, for example, does Leggatt strip off *all* his clothes to swim? This is surely unusual for the educated Englishman, the Conway Boy.[9]

Or, consider the Captain's first glimpse of him—"a headless corpse!" While Mr. Albert Guerard is certainly right in viewing Leggatt, thus imaged, as the Captain's unconscious self, it is clear (without going into psychological jargon) what aspect of the Captain's being is emphasized in Leggatt. Coming mindless from the sea (and the meaning of water in Freudian symbology need not here be elaborated), Leggatt represents a specific aspect of the unconscious life: the sexual principle: in this case, the homoerotic.

If we turn from the images and diction of the story to the characters, we see that an analysis of their development both supports the thesis that the "secret" of the story—the shared thing—is homosexuality, and that this analysis also

---

[8] Is Conrad also hinting at onanism? Notice as well the other phallic symbol, the great Paknam Pagoda, later used with double significance on his voyage (as we now understand it), "to take a compass bearing of" (p. 25).

[9] Or why, when he comes aboard, does the Captain dress him in pajamas?

"The garb of the unconscious life" has become a critical cliché: the ambiguity is at once more obvious, and (until now) more obscure. There is, of course, in the following action of the story, no reason why Leggatt should not be given a full suit of clothing. However, he seems to wear the sleeping suit always (p. 29).

leads to a fuller interpretation of the work within the archetype I have called the Hyacinthine. Aside from Leggatt and
the Captain, the only personages given fictional development
are Archbold, the Steward, and the Chief Mate. All of these
people are seen as ridiculous at best, threatening or viciously
uncomprehending at worst.

The Chief Mate is virtually a figure of fun. But why?
He is earnest, a good seaman: virtues which the mariner
Conrad should have approved of. An examination of the
devices through which he is made ridiculous is revealing.
The terms are reiterated, if anything, too much. The Mate
has "frightful whiskers" (p. 5). The Captain trifles with the
"terrific character of his whiskers" (p. 18). The Mate with the
"terrific whiskers" (p. 28). His "terrific whiskers" (p. 29). "The
mate's whiskers became much concerned" (p. 30). "The
moral [!] support of his whiskers" (p. 34).

In short, it is entirely by emphasis upon this secondary
masculine sexual characteristic that the mate is ridiculed.
His very obvious bluff and hearty masculinity is his "fictional
crime" which in Burkean terms makes him eligible for our
contempt.[10]

As for Archbold, who is even more strongly ridiculed,
his defects are also of the same order. He is masculine; he
is good solid middle class, law abiding, and fitting into the
normal social and heterosexual pattern. He wishes to follow
the ways of law and order, and in the terms of the story
(properly interpreted) this is suspect.[11] But his biggest
fictional crime is that he is happily married—" 'Oh yes!' "
says Leggatt, " 'she's [the wife] on board' " the *Sephora*,
Archbold's ship.

The Steward is a rather more complex and puzzling
figure. He is, on the level of action story as well as archetype and symbol, the most threatening personage to the
Captain. It is he who scares the Captain the most, for

[10] It is no contradiction that it might
also mask a hidden esteem or envy on the
part of the Captain. (Notice also on p. 9,
that Leggatt has "no growth on his
cheeks").

[11] By contrast to the narrator, he is "a
very nice man" (p. 23) in the opinion
of the heterosexual Chief Mate.

example by hanging the Captain's coat in the bathroom[12] (p. 27) and by hearing Leggatt in the cabin (p. 25). The Steward is indeed the one who could bring "the disaster of discovery. It hung like a sword over our heads" (p. 26).

But this is very largely a threat at the level of action story, and the critics who have failed to perceive the true nature of the secret shared by Leggatt and the Captain have nevertheless perceived that the story has a far deeper meaning than one of action. On that level, the Steward in one sense combines the mother and father images in his very domesticity of cook and masculine sailor, while yet hinting at the nature of the secret by combining these two elements.

Even more importantly, he is the very archetype of the fussy, nonplussed father, sensing something strange in his son but not knowing quite what to do. His concern, his baffled solicitude, then represent, on a deeper level, both the threat of exposure to Leggatt and the Captain, and an appeal and temptation to the Captain to return to more socially accepted and acceptable ways. This is why the Steward represents the Sword hanging over the Captain's head, the most dangerous of threats.[13] The ambiguity is one of Conrad's most adroit.

In short, then, all the antithetical characters in the story[14] are depicted as such in dramatic terms that emphasize their masculinity and acceptance of the normal sexual and/or social order. This is their true meaning, although not necessarily Conrad's intended meaning.

So much for an analysis of *why* the story should be interpreted as having the secret of homosexuality. Its real meaning lies in its relationship to the Hyacinthine archetype,

---

[12] The "secret place" of the adolescent—and where Leggatt is then hidden.

[13] For a discussion of Conrad's use of a knife (not sword) as a Freudian phallic symbol in *Victory*, see Moser, pp. 117–118.

[14] Is the "young cub" of a second mate whose eye once catches that of the Captain, only to have the Captain look down (p. 4), and who is even younger than Leggatt and the Captain, a precursor of Leggatt? Is he Rosaline to Leggatt's Juliet? He also disappears from the story after this brief introduction. Note that he is the only other character who is more than mentioned in the story. The crew itself is made up of faceless men.

for it is only in the re-experiencing of the archetype that we can come to terms with life. In so far as the Captain *is* everyman and Leggatt *is* his double, in these mythic terms, the Captain *is* Apollo and Leggatt *is* Hyacinth. Space does not permit a full recounting of the myth here: it suffices to say that Hyacinth was a comely youth who was loved by Apollo. The love was returned, but it was to have a fatal consequence. Apollo accidentally killed Hyacinth while the two were sporting with discuses or quoits.

Naturally, Conrad cannot follow the archetype exactly, for then there would be only one story, not two. But the myth underlies "The Secret Sharer" and informs it with fictional power. Conrad has dreamed what "exists" and hence has dreamed the archetypal story, which is the more powerful for its lack of closeness to the original myth.

Leggatt and the Captain come together and "sport" as in the first "bed scene" referred to above. They share their secret against the outer world, but as in the archetype it cannot be sustained.

Notice the terms in which Leggatt protests against the outer world of his parson-father and the twelve jurymen and the judge. "What can they know whether I am guilty or not" he says (p. 29)—which of course is nonsense on one level, since he was found with his hands locked around another's throat.[15] That is, it is nonsense until he subtly adds: "or of *what* I am guilty either? That's my affair." We realize then that the inhabitants of one world are expressing the equality and perhaps even superiority of their *mores* over the "safe and sound" social structure of the

---

[15] Conrad subtly shifts his original materials (thereby calling our attention to the original) by suppressing the real-life fact that the victim was a Negro. This irresistibly calls to mind the myths of racial sexual superiority present in our society today, together with the special night club, the café, the black and tan joint; for the meaning of a story of this complexity is not restricted to the significance of the historical meaning which it had for its first readers, or indeed to the meaning possible in the fictional date of its action. That our present sociological patterns could not have been known to Conrad or the readers of his story, in no way influences the meaning of the work of art to its present readers.

Archbolds. Again Conrad is far in advance of his Edwardian times.

Just after this point the Captain explains their constant whispering, as he never does the sleeping-suit. "In the same whisper, as if we two whenever we talked had to say things to each other which were not fit for the world to hear," he says. (He is not so sure of himself as Leggatt, but notice he speaks not only of "understanding" but also of compulsion: not "had things to say" but "had to say things.") At this juncture Leggatt breathes out, "It's very wonderful" (p. 29).

As Leggatt is about to leave the ship, to swim toward the black hill of Kohring, the towering fragment (and phallic symbol, rounding off the image structure, by referring us back to the Paknam Pagoda) of the desolate island, again the secret is enacted. They are parting in the Captain's cabin, about to make their way to the sail-locker. The Captain's words have a clear tone which if taken out of context and placed in a "romantic" novel about a girl and a boy would not jar: "Our eyes met; several seconds elapsed, till, our glances still mingled, I extended my hand and turned the lamp out" (p. 33).

In the archetype, of course, Leggatt is killed, but by skillful variation Conrad only threatens the death of Leggatt through the Captain's actions. The rocky shore threatens the death of both men, Leggatt-Hyacinth and Captain-Apollo. The ship is all but wrecked (as if the discus threatens to boomerang) and Leggatt is all but killed in the surf.[16]

The scene in the sail-locker, then, is not only the archetype of Jonah and the Whale and the Cain-Abel myths as Mr. Louis Leiter asserts,[17] but is a simulacrum of the relationship between the men just as clearly as Gerald's and

---

[16] For the critics seem to forget that if the surf and rock are such that they could possibly wreck a large sailing vessel, they could certainly pound to bits the body of a man clad—as always—only in a sleeping suit.

[17] *Critics*, pp. 147-150. Mr. Leiter sees that "the sail-locker scene is crucial to . . . the functioning of the archetypal patterns. . . . Until the transfer of the hat, Cain, Abel, Jonah, and the scapegoat relationship are mingled and fused into each other." But he does not trace the Hyacinthine myth.

Birkin's wrestling is in D. H. Lawrence's *Women in Love.*
Even the diction of the passage supports the interpretation:

> We were in the sail-locker, scrambling on our knees over
> the sails. A sudden thought struck me. . . . I snatched off
> my floppy hat and tried hurriedly in the dark to *ram* it
> on my other self. He dodged and fended off silently . . .
> and suddenly desisted. Our hands met gropingly, lingered
> united in a steady motionless clasp. . . . No word was
> breathed by either of us when they separated. (p. 33,
> italics supplied)

And, finally, making his meaning trebly clear, after Leggatt
has left the ship, the Captain's penultimate thought of
Leggatt is not of Leggatt *qua* Leggatt or all of Leggatt.
By this I mean that the hat, the significance of which has
troubled so many critics, is viewed by the Captain as "the
expression of my sudden pity [i.e., fellow feeling for and
identification with] his mere [i.e., only his] flesh."[18]

There remains only the closing paragraph of the story.
This has always puzzled critics, for they cannot quite account for it in the story's terms. Mr. Guerard is a good
example—the separateness of the two characters in the last
paragraph does not quite fit his interpretation of the story
as the archetypal night journey.

> In psychological terms the positive end of the introspec-
> tive experience is incorporation, not separation and split.
> But such an end would have required Leggatt to remain
> on board indefinitely, an absurdity in dramatic if not
> psychological terms.

The ending is a kind of "desperate hope" on Conrad's or the
narrator's part.[19]

Only in terms of the Hyacinthine archetype can the last
paragraph be properly explicated. So complex is this story
that the paragraph has a double or triple significance, over-

---

[18] As we must read Yeats's "mere anarchy
is loosed" as meaning that there is only
anarchy in the modern world. Cf. "The
Second Coming." (Quoted from memory,
as the University's *Variorium Yeats* is
unavailable and my own library is still
crated from a recent removal.)

[19] I have drastically abbreviated Mr.
Guerard's account. See *Critics,* pp. 66–69.

lapping and coruscating meanings. There is the meaning of Conrad the Anglo-Polish seaman, and of the conscious Captain, and perhaps unconscious meanings on the part of both the author and the narrator.

But the reader knows, in the light of the foregoing analysis, that when the Captain *seems* to be thinking of the sharer of his secret and his cabin as a "free man, a proud swimmer striking out for a new destiny," that his tone belies the surface significance of the passage. What the Captain is really *feeling*, whether he or Conrad is fully aware of it or not, is: "Come back to the ship ag'in, Leggatt Honey!"

—Bruce Harkness

Mrs. Bennet and the
Dark Gods:
The Key to Jane Austen

❧ Although our age has witnessed the superseding of tame traditional criticism by the anthropological-psychological method, the study of Jane Austen has not yet caught up with the new movement. Her critics still talk about "social comedy" and "eighteenth-century rationality" and the like. The revolutionary exponents of archetypal myth, who have revealed unsuspected depths in many familiar works of literature, have quite failed to see Jane Austen's essential affinity with Melville and Kafka.

That her mythic patterns should have gone so long unrecognized is startling evidence of the real subtlety of her mind and art, which have been so much praised for shallow reasons. Even a brief examination of the occult structuring of *Pride and Prejudice* will establish Jane Austen's claim to be the first great exemplar of the modern mythic consciousness. If conventional criticism should object that she was a notably rational person, and that she had read little outside eighteenth-century belles lettres, it may be said in reply that it is of the essence of the mythic technique that it should be at least half unconscious, that its operations should disclose themselves only to the anthropological critic. It may be granted that the various myths which underlie the smooth and simple surface of *Pride and Prejudice* are not fully and organically developed but—in keeping with the fragmentariness of the modern psyche and its world—are only momentarily touched or blended in nebulous and shifting configurations; yet their presence in depth re-creates the values implicit in the outwardly commonplace situations of genteel village life. In mythic criticism the great thing is to find some semi-submerged rocks to stand on.

To the average casual reader, the first short chapter of *Pride and Prejudice* appears only to state the common theme of love and marriage, to set forth the character and situation of Mr. and Mrs. Bennet and their five marriageable daughters, and to report the arrival in the neighborhood of a highly eligible young bachelor, Mr. Bingley. Yet, from this brief and supposedly comic exposition, hints of the mythic and even mystic emerge. The famous first sentence, "It is a truth universally acknowledged, that a single man in possession of a good fortune must be in want of a wife," goes far beyond surface literalness. For on the next page we are told that Mrs. Bennet had been a beauty, and the single man in want of a wife reflects that desire for perpetuation of beauty expounded in Plato's *Symposium*. Ironically, although Mrs. Bennet has, in Platonic language, experienced "birth in beauty" five times, only one of her daughters is really beautiful; but it is this one that soon attracts Bingley.

Further, who and what is Bingley, the mysterious, ebullient stranger from the north who descends with his band of followers (his two sisters and Mr. Hurst and Mr. Darcy) upon a sleepy, conventional society and whom young people at once look to for providing dances? Clearly he is Dionysus, the disturbing visitor from northern Thrace. And who then is Pentheus, the king of Thebes who resisted the newcomer and was torn to pieces by the Maenads led by his own mother? Such violent data had to be somewhat adjusted by the author, yet it is hardly less clear that Pentheus is Mr. Bennet, the king of his small domain who is resentful of strangers and professedly unwilling to call on Bingley (his lack of tragic integrity is betrayed by his actually calling), and who undergoes a symbolic death in that he has no son and that his estate is entailed. Mrs. Bennet, to be sure, is not responsible for the entail, but she nags about it constantly, and she has urged her husband to cultivate Bingley, so that she must be a surrogate for Pentheus' Maenad mother. Bingley's fortune is a patent transliteration of the ivy and wine of Dionysus (the family money had been acquired in trade, undoubtedly distilling); and his sudden, unexplained comings and goings correspond to the epiphanies of the god. The mythic character of Darcy and of his relation to Bingley is less certain. However, his dominating personality and his initial blindness to the charms of Elizabeth Bennet suggest the blind seer Tiresias as the mentor of Dionysus-Bingley. (I pass by the obvious homosexuality; on this level the two men are Hercules and Hylas.) Thus the simple persons and incidents of the novel take on from the start richly evocative and even sinister connotations.

As the story proceeds and tensions develop, the mythic pattern, and with it some individual roles, undergo subtle transformations; one myth shades into another. The once pretty Mrs. Bennet, whose sole concern is to get her daughters married, is an embodiment of the unthinking life-force that works through women, and she is Dionysiac in her devotion to Bingley. Her motherhood and her earthy mentality might at first suggest identification with the Earth Goddess, but one explicit clue indicates that she is the goddess of love, born of the sea—she is a native of Meryton, the town of *mare*, the sea. On this new level, Mr. Bennet is more complex and obscure, because in projecting him Miss Austen uses not so much the orthodox and familiar myth of Venus and Adonis but some Renaissance variations of it. On the one hand, in his cool indifference to his emotional wife and in his desire to be left alone in his library, Mr. Bennet is the cold Adonis, intent on his hunting, of Shakespeare's poem. On the other hand, Jane Austen fuses with this conception the Neoplatonic symbolism of Spenser's "Garden of Adonis": as an intellectual, and the parent of five daughters, Mr. Bennet is Spenser's Adonis, "the father of all Forms," and Mrs. Bennet is Spenser's Venus, simply unformed Matter. Whatever skepticism conventional scholarship may have concerning some of these interpretations, no one could dispute this last point.

But the security of Venus and Adonis is threatened (and will eventually be destroyed) by the Boar. In Jane Austen's multiple layers of meaning, the Boar is the entail, which comes into force with Mr. Bennet's death and which is personified in his heir, Rev. Mr. Collins. We have here what is perhaps the most striking mythic ambiguity in the book: Mr. Collins is both the Boar and the Bore (and his clerical status adds a further though unexploited element of traditional ritualism). Mr. Collins is in fact the axis of several polarities.

As if this interweaving of mythic patterns were not complex enough, the same pattern, with new features added, is worked out on another level and takes shape as the central figure in the carpet. The older Venus and Adonis are partly paralleled in a younger Venus and Adonis, Elizabeth and the initially proud and indifferent Darcy; but this second version operates in a vein of paradox. Mr. Bennet had in his youth been allured by a pretty face and had later discovered the stupidity behind it; Darcy, at first cold and then attracted by beauty, discovers the spirit and charm that go with it and falls deeply in love. Elizabeth, though misled for a time by the specious Wickham (a sort of Anteros), comes to love Darcy in her turn. But the security of the young pair's new relation is threatened by a variety of circumstances and most explicitly by a new Boar-Bore, not now Mr. Collins but his patroness, Lady Catherine (who has also some Gorgonish traits). Mr. Collins, like the mythical boar, while really killing had only sought to kiss (he proposed to Elizabeth); Lady Catherine, seeking to kill the relation between her nephew Darcy and Elizabeth, instead brings about his renewed proposal and acceptance. Some of these features of the design have, it is true, been noticed in conventional criticism, but only on the personal and social level; the deeper dimensions and reverberations have been completely missed.

There are many particulars one would like to go into, for instance, Elizabeth's uncle, Mr. Gardiner, whom Darcy so unexpectedly invites to fish on his estate: what is Mr. Gardiner's relation to the Fisher King, and what of the veiled phallicism in the allusion to fishing tackle?[1] But only one other thread in the variegated web of complexity can be touched upon, the most central of all archetypal myths, the theme of death and rebirth. Jane Austen's heavy reliance upon this is all the more remarkable because she is commonly said to avoid the subject of death altogether; she never has a principal character die and only rarely reports such remote deaths as may contribute to the plot. But the real reason now becomes apparent: she did not deal with the subject in ordinary ways simply because her stories of young love are set against a dark mythic background of death. In *Pride and Prejudice* hints of mortality appear at the very beginning, in such place names as Longbourn ("man goeth to his long home"; "The undiscover'd country from whose bourn No traveller returns") and Netherfield (the nether or lower world). There is a recurrent stress on physical frailty: Kitty Bennet has spells of coughing; Jane Bennet falls ill at Netherfield; Anne de Bourgh is sickly; and there is a whole crowd of adults whose parents are dead; etc. We have already observed the insistent significance of the entail and Mr. Collins, who will inherit the estate when Mr. Bennet dies. In proposing to Elizabeth, the magnanimous Mr. Collins says that he knows she will, after her mother's death, have no more than a thousand pounds in the four per cents. Such hieroglyphics of pain and death, both mythic and worldly, are reinforced by the process of the seasons. The book opens in early autumn, and in this season of harvest and death there is the ritual dance, which, ominously, takes place at Netherfield, Bingley's house. It is during the late autumn and winter that blows fall upon the Bennets—Mr.

---

[1] When the results of this inquiry were first set forth, one very obvious point was overlooked—Mr. Gardiner's relation to the first gardener, Adam. It is unthinkable that Jane Austen should not have been concerned with the theme of all literature, the Fall.

Collins' unhappy visit, Bingley's departure and abandoning of Jane Bennet and her heavy disappointment and Elizabeth's sympathy for her. The worst blow, Lydia's elopement with Wickham (note, by the way, the ancient view of the shallow, sensual quality of Lydian music), does occur in the summer, but it is this event that sets everything in motion toward rebirth, or what is crudely called a happy ending. Darcy—now a saving Hercules—rescues Lydia and wins Elizabeth; Dionysus-Bingley returns and is restored to Jane; and Mrs. Bennet, again a radiant Venus, rises from the depths in a foam of rejoicing.

Almost all the characters and incidents of the novel, under close scrutiny, will yield their mythic overtones, but perhaps enough has been said here to stimulate a critic who has the time and the insight for fuller investigation. The subject of archetypal myth in Jane Austen needs a book, and will doubtless get one.

—Douglas Bush

Eloise Disclosed

꙾ Not since the time of Swift and Rabelais has there been as cleverly disguised a piece of social commentary as the two-volume work purporting to deal with a child named (significantly enough, as we shall presently see) "Eloise." The art of concealing trenchant analysis under the cloak of alleged juvenile humor has seldom been practiced with greater dexterity; the cloak has an air of such plausibility that no critic has yet ventured to peer beneath it. Public response to the work, however, indicates that there may be a subconscious understanding of its depth among readers, but this is only an instinctive reaching-out-toward rather than a true grasping-of the meaning.

To be sure, it was virtually impossible to recognize the profound and disturbing implications of the first volume until the appearance of the second provided the necessary clues. Only then could the petals of allegory be unfolded one by one until the conception became visible as a whole; only then could it be seen that the child, Eloise, was actually devised as a surrogate for The American in Mid-Century, and that the situation in which the "child" is depicted is the brilliantly symbolic analysis of Everyman's tragic condition.

The author subtly leads us to the proper mood with the very title of the second volume (*Eloise in Paris*): the *Eloise de Paris*, though apparently only a heartrending little anagram on Eloise in *despair*, also serves to show us the direction in which the child has been moving throughout

the first volume. Looking back, we find that the whole saga
begins with what we now recognize as a *cri-de-coeur:* "I
am Eloise I am six." In this statement we are at once able
to discover the simple play on words masking the true
meaning: "I am sick." Further confirmation, if any were
needed, is found in the ending which, with a bit of technical
virtuosity reminiscent of Joyce's *Finnegans Wake,* brings
the narrative to full circle with a double reiteration of the
illness theme, first disguised as a sham sickness ("And Nanny
has to get up and pamper me . . . while I am out of my
head with fever and pain"), then returning to the original
word-play with an added note of pathos: "After all I am
only six" (sick). The symbolic child, like her prototype,
cannot bring herself to more than a dim, peripheral realization of her condition.

We know, then, of the existence of this illness; but what
is its nature? This, as one might suspect, is a more difficult
problem in view of the fact that all knowledge of the illness
itself is repressed. One must deduce from negative evidence.
What, one asks, is the salient *lack* in the luxurious and
frenetic life of this child? The answer is at once apparent:
she is living *without a mother,* a deprivation made the more
poignant by her complete failure to recognize it as such.
Yet this is the problem only in its most superficial sense.
What is the deeper meaning? Given our understanding of
the author's deft sense of word-play, the answer is not
hard to find. "Mother" is simply the prosopopoeic adaptation
of its synonym, "matrix," and the problem thus exposed
is not merely that of a child's unconscious attempt to com-
pensate for the absence of a mother, but of Everyman's
desperation in the face of life without a focus, without a
matrix.

From this the allegory broadens with ineluctable logic.
We have first the child's deeply revealing matutinal rite:
"Then I . . . look at the ceiling for awhile and try to think
of a way to get a present." To the casual reader, interpreting
"present" as "gift," the phrase would seem a puzzling one;
the child, having infinite financial credit and the latitude

to use it, obviously has no need of gifts. However, following the deeper theme, we realize that this word indicates that Everyman, finding his *present* life untenable, is desperately seeking some alternative to the "nothingness" that surrounds him. (Note here the artful interweaving of the Existentialist theme as in Heidegger's *"Das nichts nichtet"* and Sartre's *"Je suis mon propre néant."*)

Granting the terrible emptiness of life without a matrix, where is our protagonist to turn? This question brings us to the very heart of the author's incisive analysis. We have penetrated the underbrush and are at last in sight of the fundamental point: retroactive tropism. Seen in this light the child's telephonic cathexis is not merely an aimless evasion, but a dynamic and purposeful little ballet of flight. What is it that she seeks when, in every crisis, she turns to the telephone? What does she hope to find at "the end of the line"? It is René, the waiter who, now that we have the key, is obviously her yearning to be *reborn* (*re-né*) into a new and different life. At once the umbilical function of the telephone cord becomes apparent, and the punning conversion of the womb and its cervical passage into "room service" is so obvious as to approach vulgarity.

Hanging as she is in the limbo between an untenable present and an unfulfillable dream of the past, Eloise (the lost child in everyone) is naturally engaged in a desperate ego-drive, or struggle to find her identity. This theme is rung with delicate changes throughout both volumes, appearing first and most frequently in the reiteration: "It is me Eloise," a pathetic though gallant attempt to create an identity by simple, dogged reassertion.

Paralleling the search for identity we note the faint refrain of Everyman's transcendental aspirations in the "Nanny" figure. This symbol tends to be puzzling until we grasp the fine innuendoes of the deliberate ambiguity. In one respect "Nanny" functions as the superego ("Eloise you cawn't"), yet the clear Trinitarian implication of her propensity for saying "everything three times" marks her as an essentially religious figure. (Has the struggle to reconcile God and

Freud ever been more succinctly dramatized?) However, the small amount of security that Nanny offers in this dual capacity is scarcely sufficient to affect the child's *Weltanschauung,* or even to penetrate its hard core of skepticism. Observe the wry neological use of the letters "sk" (as in "sklathe," "skibble," "skidder," etc.) by which even the simplest of actions is colored with the hue of skepticism.

Space unfortunately does not permit a full exploration of the attitude toward the male that is so acidly sketched in these volumes. However, it is in the treatment of the male condition that the author's subjective intensity betrays his (as it must surely be) own sex; and the signature, "Kay Thompson," considered as a chosen pseudonym, hints provocatively for identification with—"Cato's Son."

Yet, illuminating as these various shafts of light may be, one is haunted by the feeling that they all come into focus at a single, as yet undisclosed point, that a magnificent flash still awaits those who have the wit to discover it. But we cannot hope to penetrate the arcanum with ease even now. We must re-examine the original picture of Eloise (Everyman) as we first saw her in the vast lobby of the "Plaza" with its great marble pillars. To this we must add the light of all we have learned of the author's brilliantly devious verbal techniques. At once it occurs to us that, in a work so rich with hidden meanings, this fundamental name, "Eloise," surely cannot be without significance. Yet the flash escapes us still until we think of applying the author's favorite device of letter-jumbling (itself so coruscatingly symbolic of the chaotic state of our times). Then at last the conception entire is presented to us in the dazzling bilingual pun-anagram: OEILLESS IN PLAZA.

—Felicia Lamport

Patristic Exegesis:
A Medieval Tom Sawyer

∽ Professors Robertson and Huppé and others, but especially the first, have offered medievalists a powerful critical tool[1] in applying the methods of scriptural exegesis to works of literature hitherto assumed to be primarily secular in intent. In Chaucer, for instance, an orthodox doctrinal core of meaning has been revealed in such unsuspected places as the *Wife of Bath's Prologue*.[2] The "patristic" method is now familiar, but a reminder of principles may not be out of place. St. Augustine announced the profoundly simple principle of interpreting Scripture: "Whatever appears in the divine Word that does not literally pertain to virtuous behavior or to the truth of faith you must take to be figurative."[3] *De Doctrina Christiana* was, of course, a work that exerted a great influence, which medieval poets could hardly have escaped. Furthermore, we have the explicit testimony of some poets like Boccaccio, who subscribed to the fruit-and-chaff theory of literature: "Fiction is a form of discourse, which, under guise of invention, illustrates or proves an idea; and, as its superficial aspect is removed, the meaning

[1] See particularly D. W. Robertson, Jr., *A Preface to Chaucer* (Princeton, 1962), and Bernard F. Huppé and D. W. Robertson, Jr., *Fruyt and Chaf* (Princeton, 1963).

[2] Also in the *Miller's Tale, Nun's Priest's Tale*, etc.

[3] *On Christian Doctrine*, 3.14, trans. D. W. Robertson, Jr. (Indianapolis, 1958).

of the author is clear. If, then, sense is revealed from under the veil of fiction, the composition of fiction is not idle nonsense."[4] To be sure, Boccaccio does not say that the kernel beneath the husk must pertain to virtuous behavior or to the truth of faith; but with the knowledge that all medieval poets were orthodox Christians,[5] we may safely assume the *nucleus* of fiction to be sound doctrine. Essentially there is but one doctrine, and again it is profoundly simple: "Scripture teaches nothing but charity, nor condemns anything except cupidity."[6] "I call 'charity' the motion of the soul toward the enjoyment of God for His own sake, and the enjoyment of one's self and of one's neighbor for the sake of God; but 'cupidity' is a motion of the soul toward the enjoyment of one's self, one's neighbor, or any corporal thing for the sake of something other than God."[7]

Since this is the sole theme of medieval literature, some interesting reinterpretations of that literature are implied. Thus all "love" stories, insofar as they portray cupidinous "love," are ironic *exempla* condemning the foolishness and vice to which unbridled concupiscence leads. Certain aesthetic revaluations must also follow. The *De Amore* of Andreas Capellanus, for instance, by no means so stupefying as it appears to be, is actually, as Professor Robertson, with a fine sense of humor, says, "hilarious." Even the *Miller's Tale* has a sober "sentence," at bottom.

Aesthetically, medieval literature is intellectual, never emotional; we must constantly be on our guard against reading modern romanticism into medieval literature. The appeal of the *Chanson de Roland, Guy of Warwick,* and *Beves of Hamtoun* is purely intellectual; it has absolutely nothing to do with the sentimental moonshine of a Kafka, T. S. Eliot, or Mary McCarthy, whose aesthetics are so dominated by Schlegel and the *Indian Love Lyrics.*

The soundness of the whole approach is obvious, though

[4] Quoted in *Fruyt and Chaf,* p. 20.

[5] Some monks and priests were, paradoxically, less reliable, such as Peter Abelard, Arnold of Brescia, Siger of Brabant.

[6] *On Christian Doctrine,* 3.10.15.

[7] *Ibid.,* 3.10.16.

there are those who will probably continue to shake their heads over the strange doctrines which permeated the mores and *amores* of the Middle Ages. What I propose to show here is that this critical tool is actually more powerful and far-reaching than heretofore realized. Clearly there is no a priori reason to draw an arbitrary historical line beyond which the method does not apply. Quite the contrary, we still live in a Christian world, and the Augustinian tradition has continued unbroken. Indeed, Augustine was and is the "patron saint" of the Reformation and Calvinism; and American Protestantism, thus, has been the direct heir of this tradition. We must not be deceived by modern illusions about historical time; it should be remembered that Mark Twain is six centuries closer to Chaucer than Chaucer to St. Augustine, and if Chaucer's debt to the Fathers is not completely documented, we *do* know that Twain had read Chaucer. Let us consider, then, Chapter Eight of *The Adventures of Tom Sawyer.* The first thing the reader sees is this:

8

 Tom Decides on His Course
—Old Scenes Re-enacted

Any reader raised in the Augustinian tradition (Twain was brought up a Presbyterian) would immediately recognize that the number 8 signifies the resurrection and salvation.[8] In the chapter title itself, Twain unmistakably points to a moral decision to be based, in this Christian context, precisely on traditional typology. Thus Twain's contemporary readers would be prepared by the chapter heading for a serious allegorical *sententia* behind the apparently frivolous

---

[8] See Rabanus, *De Universo, P.L.*, 111.491; Bede, *De templo Salmonis, P.L.,* 91.806; Gregory *P.L. 76* 1341, 1391; Lombard, *P.L.* 191.103; Augustine, *Contra Faustum,* 16.29, *Civ. Dei,* 15.20, and Letter 55, 13.23.

littera of the text, an expectation, which, as we shall see, is strikingly fulfilled.

Slighted by Becky Thatcher, Tom, in a morose state of mind, has played hooky and gone off to the woods:

> He entered a dense wood, picked his pathless way to the center of it, and sat down on a mossy spot under a spreading oak. There was not even a zephyr stirring; the dead noonday heat had even stilled the songs of the birds; nature lay in a trance that was broken by no sound but the occasional far-off hammering of a woodpecker, and this seemed to render the pervading silence and sense of loneliness the more profound. The boy's soul was steeped in melancholy; his feelings were in happy accord with his surroundings. He sat long with his elbows on his knees and his chin in his hands, meditating. It seemed to him that life was but a trouble, at best, and he more than half envied Jimmy Hodges, so lately released; it must be very peaceful, he thought, to lie and slumber and dream forever and ever, with the wind whispering through the trees and caressing the grass and the flowers over the grave, and nothing to bother and grieve about, ever any more. If he only had a clean Sunday-school record he could be willing to go, and be done with it all.

No reader of Chaucer can fail to recognize the situation. It is precisely that of the Man in Black in the *Book of the Duchess*.

> But forth they romed ryght wonder faste
> *Doun the woode*; so at the laste
> I was war of a man in blak,
> That sat and had yturned his bak
> To an *ook*, an huge tree.
> "Lord," thoght I, "who may that be?"   (442-8)[9]

Like the narrator of the *Book of the Duchess,* Tom is in a wood. Like Dante too—"mi retrovai per una selva oscura, che la diritta via era smaritta"—he is in "a dense wood," a "pathless way," a *forest espesse* like the heroes of Cretien.[10]

[10] Cf. Manfred Gsteiger, *Die Landschafts-schilderungen in den Romanen Chrestiens de Troyes* (Bern, 1958), p. 18.

[9] References to Chaucer are to F. N. Robinson's edition (Boston, 1957). Italics added.

The "dense wood" is a commonplace symbol for the life of this world.[11] Thus Tom's situation is that of mankind—but mankind in particular circumstances, for, like the Man in Black, he sits under the oak of despair.[12] The symbolic language gives us a further clue as to the psychology[13] of the protagonist. He has gone a "pathless way." Since *semita* means *cogitatio*,[14] the "pathless way" represents a divagation from the higher reason (or, which is the same thing, "separatio ab Ecclesia"[15]); that is, the lower reason, traditionally associated with women,[16] has overpowered the masculine higher reason. In the *De Trinitate* (12:12), Augustine, giving a tropological account of the Fall, equates Adam with "the higher part of the reason whose function is *sapientia,* or wisdom, and Eve represents the lower part of the reason, whose function is *scientia,* or knowledge of things seen. . . . In this context, the serpent represents the motion of the senses. It tempts the lower reason which may in turn tempt the higher reason with the 'fruit' [i.e., chaff] thus presented to it."[17] This traditional division of reason into *sapientia* and *scientia* is not, of course, to be thought of as a "tension of dynamic polarities," a completely modern concept unknown to either Augustine or Twain; it is rather a typically medieval "quiet hierarchy."[18] The Oak of Despair is "spreading," that is, giving shade by its leaves. This corresponds very closely to a sermon of Hugh of St. Victor, in which he warns: "Cave ergo et tu dum sub umbra, foliorum requiem quaeris, incipias pati caliginem." The leaves are worldly

---

[11] *"Silva est* mundus iste. . . ." Rabanus Maurus, *Allegoriae, P.L.* 112.1054.

[12] *Fruyt and Chaf,* 55; Rabanus: *"Quercus* est duritia desperationis . . ." *Ibid.,* c. 1036; not to be confused with *aliquis sublimis in dignitate saeculari* or *fidelis,* or, certainly, *proprie arbor* (Alanus, *Dictinctiones, P.L.* 210.919).

[13] I.e., in its moral and philosophical significance. Modern so-called "psychological" studies regularly overlook the fact that neither Twain nor Chaucer had read Freud (see *Preface,* 36).

[14] *P.L.* 210.940.

[15] *Ibid.*

[16] *Preface,* passim.

[17] *Ibid.,* 74.

[18] As illustrated by Augustine, for example, speaking of the quiet hierarchy of flesh and spirit: "Tunc ergo coepit *caro concupiscere adversus spiritum* [Gal. 5.17], cum qua controversia nati sumus, trahentes originem mortis et in membris nostris vitiataque natura contentionem eius sive victoriam de prima praevaricatione gestantes." (*Civ. Dei,* 13.13)

knowledge, which is vanity, shutting off spiritual light: "Sed tamen dum stant, umbram faciunt et habent refrigerium suum; sed est obscura umbra et inimica lumini"; "this light is the sunshine of God's justice":[19] "lunen verae sapientiae, apud quam stultitia est sapientia iste (sc. scientia), videre non possunt."[20]

The symbolism of the first sentence is amplified in the next. The "noonday heat" is described as "dead." This is more than merely a striking metaphor; the "noonday heat" obviously represents the light and warmth of God's justice, or *vera sapientia,* from which Tom is cut off by the spreading Oak of Despair, and is therefore "dead" to Tom, or Tom is "dead" to it. Death in this context has the traditional meaning of slavery to vice, i.e., cupidity (*cupidinis vincula*), as Chaucer's Parson says, "He is ded whil that he liveth in tho vices." We observe further that the songs of the birds have been stilled (cf. the Man in Black "Withoute noote, withoute song"). Traditionally, the singing of birds is a celebration of God's love, a *novum canticum* reflecting the celestial harmony.[21] Here they are significantly silent, except for the sound of the *woodpecker.* The libidinous connotations of *woodpecker* are too obvious to require comment.[22] *Charitas,* then, is silent, and only *cupiditas* is heard, suggesting again the nature of Tom's despair, a suggestion subsequently verified, as we shall see.

Now again like the Man in Black, Tom is "steeped in melancholy" and contemplates suicide. Cf. Chaucer:

> "I have of sorwe so gret won
> That joye gete I never non,   (475–6)
> .... Allas, deth, what ayleth the,
> That thou noldest have taken me."   (481–2)

[19] D. W. Robertson, Jr., "The Doctrine of Charity in Mediaeval Literary Gardens: A Topical Approach through Symbolism and Allegory," *Speculum,* 26 (1951), 26.

[20] *Hom. IX in Eccles., P.L.* 175.171-2, quoted by Robertson, *loc. cit.* (The twenty-eight meanings of *umbra* and *folium* given by Rabanus and Alanus are not relevant in this context.)

[21] *P.L.* 210.1009. Cf. St. Ambrose, *Hexameron, P.L.* 14.237-8; Gregory, *Moralia, P.L.* 76.97.

[22] Twain may also have been thinking of the fact that *picus* sometimes translates *grupos,* "griffin," a traditional symbol of wickedness. On bird-lore in general see Robertson's learned notes in *Preface,* 411.

But that Tom's despair is not total is shown by his rejection of the idea of suicide, a victory of *sapientia,* which contemplates "things unseen," in this case "drede of domesday": *"If he only had a clean Sunday-school record* he could be willing to go, and be done with it all." (Italics added.) Thus his awareness of sin leads him to the first step of penitence, foreshadowing the final resolution of the chapter.

The cause of despair in both the *Book of the Duchess* and *Tom Sawyer* is, as we have been led to suspect, cupidinous "love." Both the Man in Black and Tom are plunged into despair by the loss of a "beloved" female.

> "I have of sorwe so gret won
> That joye gete I never non,
> Now that I see my lady bryght,
> Which I have loved with all my myght,
> Is fro me ded and ys agoon."   (475–9)

"Now, as to this girl. What had he done? Nothing. He had meant the best in the world, and been treated like a dog— like a very dog. She would be sorry some day—maybe when it was too late." No better comment on the significance of these parallel passages can be given than that of Professors Huppé and Robertson:

> The true reason for his sorrow is error; the speaker had been temporarily misled to believe that the loss of another human was the cause of his grief. In Christian fact there can be no sorrow except that arising in separation from God. A man's love has two sides, one false (cupidity), the other true (charity); his grief has two sides, one *tristitia,* false grief caused by the loss of an object of desire, the other a true grief caused by his enforced bodily separation from God. What the speaker had taken as grief was itself false worldly vanity.[23]

Tom's wallowing in self-pity is expressly a romantic delusion: "The idea of being a clown recurred to him now, only to fill him with disgust. For frivolity and jokes and spotted tights were an offense, when they intruded themselves upon a spirit that was exalted into the vague realm of the *roman-*

[23] *Fruyt and Chaf.,* 55.

tic." (Italics added.) However, his higher reason is still operative, as we have seen, and he is accessible to Grace. He is roused from his melancholy and despair by the sound of a horn: "Just here the blast of a toy tin trumpet came faintly down the green aisles of the forest." Again, the parallel to the *Book of the Duchess* is striking.

> And as I lay thus, wonder lowde
> Me thought I herde an hunte blowe
> T'assay hys horn, . . .   (344–6)

On which Huppé and Robertson comment judiciously, "He hears the horn of hope sounding the call of the hunt of Christ and His Church for the human soul."[24] *Sonus* is aptly explained by Alanus: "Dicitur etiam inspiratio divina quae, mediante homine, pugnat contra diabolum, peccatum et mundum; unde David: *Laudate eum in sono tubae,* id est in eo quod, divina inspiratione mediante, sancti vincunt diabolum, id est vitia; tuba enim invitamur ad bellum, etc."[25] So Tom is called to the struggle against his *vitia*. Moreover, as we have seen, Tom, aware of his spotty Sunday-school record, is prepared for penitence. As the Parson says, quoting St. Ambrose, "Penitence is the waymentynge of man that sorweth for his synne, and pyneth himself for he hath misdoon." Hence the traditional meaning *gemitus poeniten-tiae*[26] for *sonus* also fits our context. Tom's reaction to the sound of the horn is that of a faithful Christian: "Tom flung off his jacket and trousers, turned a suspender into a belt, raked away some brush behind the rotten log, disclosing a rude bow and arrow, a lath sword and a tin trumpet, and in a moment had seized these things and bounded away, barelegged, with fluttering shirt. . . . Now appeared Joe Harper, as airily clad and elaborately armed as Tom."

This is a passage particularly rich in scriptural symbolism and allusion. First, there is a suggestion in Tom's throwing off his jacket and trousers of that *nudus* referred to by

[24] *Ibid.*, 97.
[25] *P.L.* 210.949.
[26] *P.L.* 112.1059.

Alanus when he says, "Greg. ait quod nudi debemus luctari
cum diabolo."[27] The girding of the loins with a belt and
the taking up of arms obviously echo Eph. 6.11–17: "State
ergo succincti lumbros vestros in veritate. . . . adsumite et
gladium spiritus, quod est verbum Dei." As the sword is
verbum Dei likewise the bow and arrow are *sermo Dei* or
sacrae Scripturae sententia.[28] All together these weapons
constitute the Christian's *arma*: "Dicitur etiam doctrina,
ut in *Psalmo: Apprehendite arma,* id est doctrinam."[29]
Though "doctrine" is the primary meaning of *arma* in this
context, as we shall see, the meaning "status poenitentiam in
contritione, in confessione et in satisfactione"[30] is also suggested, answering to *sonus* as *gemitus poenitentiae.*

The several allusions to David and the Psalms have
foreshadowed the appearance of *Joe Harper,* hardly a fortui-
tous choice of names, *Harper* clearly referring to the Psalmist,
ancestor of Christ, and *Joe* to Joseph, the earthly father of
Christ.

The following exchange occurs:

> "Hold! Who comes here into Sherwood Forest without
> my pass?"
> "Guy of Guisborne wants no man's pass. Who are thou
> that—that—"
> "Dares to hold such language," said Tom, prompting—
> for they talked "by the book," from memory.

And similarly:

> "Why, that ain't anything. *I* can't fall; that ain't the
> way it is in the book. The book says, 'Then with one
> backhanded stroke he slew poor Guy of Guisborne.'
> You're to turn around and let me hit you in the back."
> There was no getting around the authorities, so Joe
> turned, received the whack and fell.

Obviously "by the book," significantly set off by quotation
marks, refers to the Scriptures; as orthodox Christians, they
are faithful to the word of God, "id est doctrina." Called,
then, by *inspiratio divina* issuing from the Psalmist, armed

[27] *P.L.* 210.877.   [29] *P.L.* 210.710–1.
[28] *P.L.* 112.1044; 210.931.   [30] *Ibid.*

with the *verbum Dei, sermo Dei,* and *doctrina,* the true *armature Dei* of the Christian, Tom is well prepared for the ensuing spiritual struggle. We need not go into the details of the combat, a commonplace of Christian tradition. It is the result that is important.

As will be recalled, the resolution of Tom's struggle with despair is forecast by the significant number of this chapter, 8, the number of resurrection and salvation. The anticipations set up in the reader by the appearance of this number at the beginning of the chapter are now clearly fulfilled. Having assumed the guise of "Robin Hood" (a familiar Christ figure), Tom has apparently lost the struggle and is dying—but only apparently: "And at last Joe, representing a whole tribe of weeping outlaws, dragged him sadly forth, gave his bow into his feeble hands, and Tom said, 'Where this arrow falls, there bury poor Robin Hood under the greenwood tree.' Then he shot the arrow and fell back *and would have died,* but he lit on a nettle *and sprang up too gaily for a corpse."* (Italics added.) The pattern of death and resurrection is evident to anyone. Thus, a true *miles Christi,* Tom has responded to his *vocatio* to undertake an *imitatio Christi.* It may well be that the name *Sawyer* is meant to recall that Christ was a carpenter. *Allegorice,* Tom represents Christ; tropologically, the lesson of the chapter is obviously that as Christ escaped the bondage to this world, *cupiditas,* by a motion of the soul toward God, so to each Christian who rejects *concupiscentia, cupiditas,* and *duritia desperationis,* the way to salvation is open.

It appears likely from this analysis that Twain knew *and understood* the *Book of the Duchess.* In any case, it is perfectly clear that Twain belongs in the tradition of Christian humanistic literature. Modern critics, hoodwinked by romantic sentimentality, will no doubt persist in seeing *Tom Sawyer* as "only a boy's book," but the deeper message is obvious: under the apparently frivolous *cortex* of this extraordinary work there is a profound condemnation of the foolishness and vice to which unbridled concupiscence leads.

—John Halverson

Six, Sex, Sick:
Seymour, Some Comments

∽ In the deluge of Salinger criticism the critics have spoken learnedly of Rilke, Dostoyevsky, Twain and Buddha, they have fallen over crazy cliffs and looked intently through dark glasses hoping to see more literary allusions; but, they have neglected "Little Black Sambo." Poor "Sambo," suffering the curse of the academically forgotten, silently holds an important key to "A Perfect Day for Bananafish."

Sybil (the prophetess) Carpenter, the yellow bathing-suit-clad little girl in "Bananafish," gives a veiled clue to the story's meaning. The prophetess speaks:

> "Did you read 'Little Black Sambo'?" she said. "It's very funny you asked me that," he said. "It so happens I just finished reading it last night." He reached down and took back Sybil's hand. "What did you think of it?" he asked her. "Did the tigers run all around that tree?" "I thought they'd never stop. I never saw so many tigers." "There were only six," Sybil said. "*Only* six!" said the young man. "Do you call that *only*?"[1]

The number six is an important key to "Bananafish's" interpretation, and, indeed, to the moral and psychological problems of Seymour. As a matter of fact, there are really four tigers, not six, in the children's "Sambo." Salinger

[1] J. D. Salinger, *Nine Stories* (New York, 1954), p. 15.

had made a change, and we can trust that it is a conscious and not inadvertent change. For Salinger, the aspostle of salvation by child (NB: *The Catcher in the Rye;* "Uncle Wiggily in Connecticut;" "Down by the Dinghy"; "For Esme—with Love and Squalor") would hardly inadvertently make such an error.

In "Bananafish" (1948), Seymour and Muriel Glass have been married for six years, a fact not revealed in Salinger's gradual unfolding of the Glass family's chronicle until *Raise High the Roof Beam, Carpenters* (1955). Seymour is the most admirable figure in Salinger's fiction, a fact well developed in Salinger's latest efforts,[2] for in him is combined the intellect of a genius and the moral sensitivity and compassion of a Buddhist monk; his six years with Muriel ("Miss Spiritual Tramp of 1948") have been a failure. The marriage has been six years of tigerish pride, vanity, and selfishness, in which their souls and the spiritual communion of their marriage have melted, like Sambo's tigers, into rancid nothingness.

The six-tiger image also gives a clue as to the nature of Seymour's spiritual evisceration and as to why he commits suicide. Their sixth anniversary is being spent in Miami Beach, the glittering home of the superannuated and the depraved, the symbol of the jaded Muriel and a world that runs in circles after the tigers of crass materialism and superficiality. In the hotel room Muriel reads "Sex [Latin, six] Is it Fun or Hell"—in Seymour's case Hell—and leaves her wedding ring in the bathroom while she dries her nail polish and blandly holds a telephone conversation with her mother, both of them giving equal emphasis to topics ranging from Seymour's mental breakdown to new fashions. For the hypersensitive like Seymour there is a horror in a mother-in-law who lumps his breakdown ("It's horrible") and Muriel's sunburn ("that's terrible") into the same category, and a wife who discusses his problems with a psychiatrist in the hotel bar ("It was terribly noisy.").

[2] See: J. D. Salinger, *Raise High the Roof Beam, Carpenters* and *Seymour, An Introduction* (Boston, 1962).

The number six also gives meaning to the rather puzzling title of "Bananafish," something about which there has been much critical controversy.[3] Sybil earns her name by seeing clearly the situation and by prophesying the doom that will be Seymour's.

> "... I just saw one."
> "Saw what, my love?"
> "A bananafish."
> "My God, no!" said the young man.
> "Did he have any bananas in his mouth?"
> "Yes," said Sybil, "Six."[4]

Apart from the obvious priapic symbolism of the six bananas in reference to the six years of marriage, the banana is also symbolic as the gross, material, sensual existence that engorges the bananafish (Seymour) and is epitomized in moral degradation of Miami Beach society. As is the case with the bloated fish, Seymour gets "banana fever" and dies, but physically as well as spiritually.

The suicide itself continues the theme of number six; for Seymour in "Bananafish" there is no apotheosis as in *Seymour, An Introduction* (1959), but he merely rises in the elevator to room 507. Here, he shoots himself and ends the sixth year of his marriage which, like the middle, missing integer in the room number series, is synonymous with zero, a total void.

From the Seymour of 1942, the brave, virile Ares ("Raise high the roof beam, carpenters. Like Ares comes the bridegroom, taller far than a tall man."),[5] the carpenter image has come full cycle. In 1948 Seymour is no longer the *toro bravo* Ares, the vigorous lover of Aphrodite, he is the inglorious goat ("I'm Capricorn. . . . What are you?"). The image is clear, for in classic mythology Capricorn was once Pan, who through fear of Typhon, changed himself into a

[3] See: W. Weigand, "J. D. Salinger; Seventy-Eight Bananas." *Chicago Review*, XI (Winter, 1958), pp. 3–19, and F. Z. Gwynn and J. L. Boltner, *The Fiction of J. D. Salinger* (Pittsburgh, 1958), pp. 19–21.

[4] "Bananafish," p. 17.

[5] *Raise High the Roof Beam, Carpenters*, p. 76.

goat. Muriel and the six, deadly years of marriage are Seymour's Typhon, and these morally malignant forces have spiritually and emotionally emasculated Salinger's Pan image.

By using the number six as both a focal point and a point of departure, Salinger has created a Seymour who must destroy his physical being as the "bananas" have destroyed his soul; he cannot live in a Miami Beach world where wives neglect Rilke ("He [Seymour] said I should've bought a translation or something. Or *learned the language, if you please.*"), and have their hair "dyed mink." It is Seymour's "Wasteland," and "mixing memory with desire,"[6] the pure, spring rain of the child Sharon stirs the dried tubers of his soul into the memory of the engorged bananafish that is his life.

—Charles V. Genthe

[6] T. S. Eliot, "The Wasteland," *The Wasteland and Other Poems* (New York, 1938), p. 29. And "Bananafish," p. 14.

Christian Symbolism in "Lucky Jim"

∽ At one time the attention of critics was directed in the main to work of an overtly symbolic nature. In recent years, however, we have come to see more clearly than was originally the case that writing which at a superficial level may appear to be simple or "realist" in fact provides equally valuable material for critical research.

That *Lucky Jim* is essentially a symbolic novel is now, of course, no longer disputed. Interesting work has already been done on its various levels of effect. I need only mention Professor Brezé's *Le Saveur du Néant: Essence et Existence en "Jim-la-chance"* (Paris, 1962); Dr. James Conrad's *Amis and Ariosto* (Leeds, 1959); Dr. Uruspiyev's *"Shtastlivetsat Dzhim" ot gledishteto na Marksisicheskiya Dialektik* (Sofia, 1956); Mrs. Joyce Hackensmith's *The Phallus Theme in Early Amis* (Concord, 1957); and a number of the contributions to the symposium *Essays Presented to Mr. Amis on his Fortieth Birthday* (London, 1962). Without denying the great value of the work done on such lines, it nevertheless appears that the most important, indeed central, theme of the book has not yet been adequately discussed.

It is an old story that the deepest levels of effect in our literature are often traceable to the religious elements inculcated at an early and profound level into the unconscious as well as the conscious minds of the inhabitants of our

culture. It is natural enough, therefore, that if we look
upon *Lucky Jim* as a world fable ("Weltfabel," von Lippe-
Detmold's expression)—as we must, of course, look upon
any significant work of literature—we find a pervasive tone
of religious symbolism both at the apparently superficial
verbal level (and I say "apparently" because we must not
denigrate any thread in this richly shuttled texture) and
in the basic structure of the story.

The way in which I here approach the problem is not
the only possible one. By confining myself in the main to
evidence deriving rigorously from the indisputable data of
the characters' names and tendencies, I hope it has been
possible to guard more carefully against the fanciful than
would be the case if I had permitted myself to wander freely
in the action of the book, which in the nature of things
is susceptible of more varied interpretation. Yet though
the sacrifice in scope is, it is hoped, compensated by greater
certainty in results, nevertheless we must hope that later
students will be able to grasp and illuminate the whole work
at length on the basis of this modest beginning.

Dixon, the hero, is of course Everyman. In this capacity
he is able (or required) to represent the whole human race
(from Eskimo, page 97, to Roman, page 255)—and even to
indicate the transcendental and universal scope of the God-
head by becoming briefly a Martian (page 92). (This reminds
us ineluctably—and, as we shall see, importantly—of C. S.
Lewis' religious fiction.)

But, and far more to our purpose, Dixon is also the Son
of Man. The surname, with the Cross at its centre for him
to *Di(e) on,* is among the more overt and conscious of the
many signs the author has scattered. The name Jim instant-
ly brings to mind the words of the Epistle of St. James:

> Count yourselves happy indeed, my brethren, when you
> encounter trials of every sort, as men do not know well
> enough that the testing of their faith needs endurance.
> (Monseigneur Ronald Knox's translation);

it reminds us that the Authorised Version was produced
for a king of that name: and at another level still, showing

the intricate stratification of the author's mind, it lays down
the Apocalyptic background of the whole conception, referring as it obviously does to the approaching end of the
Second Millenium (IIM), a period often designated for the
Last Things.

In a general way, the conflict between the powers of
darkness and of light is the "plot" of the novel. It is not
here my purpose to examine its scriptural ramifications. It is
sufficient to note such cruxes as the strikingly obvious beginning of Chapter 6, so extraordinary and exaggerated in
the *apparent* context of a mere awakening, but so essential
in the basic religious context—"DIXON WAS ALIVE
AGAIN"[1]—and so on, throughout. For example, in Dixon's
"lecture" we naturally find the Sermon on the Mount,
though there are other elements such as St. Paul's "speaking with tongues." (It may also be significant that in the
film version, Dixon gets his finger caught in the lectern:
that is, finds himself in effect bound to the wooden upright
with a crosspiece—an obvious enough crucifixion symbol.)

Again, it is in accord with tradition that mortals in a
state of extreme sin are unable to pronounce the holy
name. We find that the porter (page 92)—described flatly
as "a very bad man"—is unable to use Dixon's correct
name, and he substitutes "Jackson" on the analogy of the
various "odds" and "bobs" used in old expletives instead of
God. (The first syllable may represent some faint memory
of the Jewish Jehova-Yahweh substitution.)

We also cannot fail to note the pervasive echoes or rep-
resentations of the archangels. The friendly Michie is an
obvious Michael. But who can Bertrand be? The name
means "bright raven"[2] (*Origins of British Christian Names*
by J. P. Ogilvie, London, 1928, page 13), and we at once
recall the black-winged being, formerly a representation of
all light and still bearing the name Lucifer, but now an
evil spirit *par excellence*. And it is just this role that Bertrand

---

[1] Capitals in the original.

[2] We may also be reminded of the albino

rooks found by Bunyan's father in a
wood near Elstow in 1634 (*Victoria History
of Bedfordshire,* Vol. 3, p. 290).

fills at one important level. (He also has the pointed beard traditionally associated with the devil.)

The thing Dixon most resents, in his main confrontation with the bad angel, is the latter's suggestion that he (Dixon) is "Sam" (page 213). Samuel the Judge (the Gospels tell us "judge not") is the type of the Old Testament religion of power and hatred which the Christ figure has come to supersede, the man who orders the slaughter of Agag whom even the violent layman King Saul would have spared, the typo of fanaticism, the polar opposite of Dixon's mission. But more basically, we must regard this episode as representing the Satanic offer of worldly power, and its rejection.

And yet, Bertrand seems to represent only the lighter, more aerial aspects of evil. For the gross power of evil, we turn to Dixon's chief opponent, Professor "Neddy" Welch. And here we have a figure out of C. S. Lewis—evil seen as stupid and clumsy, but exceedingly powerful. "Neddy" is the hooved *animal* traditionally associated with the devil (see Chapter 3, *Traditions of Diabolism,* by J. P. Wilberforce, Hull, 1937). Welch, even if not irrevocably, rules Dixon's little world—significantly, this is the UNIVERSity. He is, in the words of *Revelations,* "Prince of this world." Reading his surname more closely we see that he is the Welt-ch. "Welt" is the "world" in German, the language of coarseness; "Ch" is, of course, the abbreviation for church (see *Ordnance Survey Abbreviations and Conventional Signs,* page 3, London, 1954). He is, in fact, an almost impersonal representation: the anti-spiritual counterpart of true religion. When Dixon enters a dark room in his house he fully expects to find him conducting some obscene satanic rite "like watching phosphorescent mould" (page 151). And we may note (page 92) that Welch is spoken of in terms of the possibility of his "being . . . conjured up" if his name is spoken. Elsewhere, Welch's features are described as "claylike" (page 9). Dixon himself, in fact, writes up the significant words that Welch has "a Fase like A Pig's Bum" (page 65). We are in the presence of the C. S. Lewis view of the impersonality of evil. Lewis expressed his Christian mythology of evil largely in science fiction form. Amis is, of course, deeply concerned with science fiction, and it is notable that his book on the subject overtly emphasises the theological in its title, *New Maps of Hell.* (It is probably no coincidence that the hero of Amis' second work is called Lewis.)

On the "evil" side, the other most prominent figure is Margaret. It is evident, and we know that Amis is a great student of sixteenth century literature (see his poem "A Note on Wyatt"), that this must be on the analogy of Marprelate.[3] But as to the precise interpretation, it must be admitted that we are not here on such certain ground. Amis on the sexual level (as Professor Hackensmith has hinted: see *New Hampshire State Literary Bulletin,* No. 3, page 277, and *Amis v. Hackensmith and Others,* New York Law Reports, 1958, pp. 1007–1026) is here entering an area of guilt and confusion, and this is reflected in obscurity at his other symbolic levels. Nevertheless, one is prepared to suggest, if tentatively, "Mar-g(ennas)areth"—omission of the One, the subject of Plotinus' *Enneads,* is itself inherently likely. That Amis regards the Biblical action round Lake Gennasereth as central is apparent in various ways; it is not for nothing that Dixon's article (pp. 14–15) is on shipbuilding. (Margaret's association with the "good pagan" Catchpole, a name that hardly needs explaining, raises issues outside the scope of this paper.)

Evan Johns, the Judas figure, is another representation of evil seen as coarse stupidity.[4] His features too are described as "junket-coloured"—those of a subterranean being who shuns the light. "Evan" is of course "heaven," deprived and mutilated. On the face of it, "Johns" might at first suggest a reference to St. John the Divine and St. John the Evangelist, and it is certainly true that Amis' conception of Christianity leans heavily on the human and charity-laden picture in the first three Gospels rather than on the more abstract,

[3] We may also think of Sir Oliver Martext, the priest (!) in *As You Like It.*
[4] His association with another "Mar" character—Marlene—must also be significant. But here I have been unable wholly to penetrate the author's intent.

semi-gnostic view taken in the Fourth or the vengeful tone of the Apocalypse. Nevertheless, one feels that it would be wrong to seek in Amis much in the way of a pursuit of a theological feud of this sort. A suggestion (by Professor Hackensmith) has a certain plausibility, though it would be premature to pronounce on it at this stage. It is that we have here another reference to the coarseness and grossness, the earthiness, of evil, and that "John" is simply the American for close-stool. It might diffidently be suggested further that the plural is not simply a modo of emphasis, but contains another "Germanic" reference, recalling the symbol with which these rooms are marked in Germany— the interlocking *double* zero, emblem of the supernullity, the extreme negativism of evil.

Christine, the representation of all that is good and beautiful in the book, is again endearingly obvious. She is of course the *Christian* Church; and the Christ figure is represented, in the oldest symbolic tradition, as heading for nuptials with her.[5] It is significant that no *gross* physical allusions are hinted at.

It has been suggested (by Dr. Conrad, pp. 113–147, op. cit.) that the "Callahan" element in her name should be taken at face value and be seen simply as a particularly coarse and rough human component, indicating that we have here the Church Militant, in its struggle with and for the ordinary human, before it becomes Triumphant and takes as its more sublime "married" name that of the Christ-figure Dixon. There is much to be said for this view, as far as it goes. But we cannot limit the many-minded Amis to a single intention even on a point like this. The Greek $\chi\alpha\lambda\alpha$ must certainly be involved. $\chi\alpha\lambda\alpha$ -han leads nowhere. *But* we note that the termination "her," a simple bridal feminine, is substituted for "han" in Dixon's telephone conversation on page 195—where a further reason for the use of a disguised accent is to enable him to say (instead of

[5] At another level, indeed, that in which Dixon is Everyman, Christine is herself Christ, the Redemption Figure, a brilliant transposition or counterpoint in the rich orchestration of Mr. Amis' theme.

"hello"), "hallaher"—as close an approximation as is plausible to "hallelujah."

Yet we cannot entirely exclude as frivolous Dr. Carlin's daring suggestion of "Colly-hen": for, as he says, these birds are traditionally associated with Christmas (as in "The First Day of Christmas," verses 3-12), and we can see that Christmas songs were not far from Amis' mind when we note the name "Carol" significantly given to one of the other sympathetic characters.

Carol is even, moreover, the wife of a singer. It is significant that his surname contains the syllable *myth*. Goldsmith has only to drop a letter—to cease to be a "*Learner*"[6]—to become "God's myth." And though in its literal significance Goldsmith appears at first sight to be a worldly, even a mammonistic profession, this is a superficial thought, for far more basically we find our attention drawn to the craftsman, the Demiourgos, who fashions the golden artefacts in Yeats' Byzantium poems ("Such a form as Grecian goldsmiths make/Of hammered gold and gold enamelling. . . .").

Progressing through the decisive figures of the book, we come at last to one whose *rôle* governs the end of the action as Welch's does the beginning. And he too is a large and taciturn figure: Gore-Urquhart. However, this time the personalisation of a more or less impersonal force is a benign one mediating the success of the Christ-figure. As against the gross "clay" of depersonalised evil, we have here a pure essence—the blood of the Lamb. The "gore" from the "heart" is obvious enough, and the only difficulty (which has misled even such students as Professor Brezé), is the "urqu." No English word begins in this manner, and we are forced at once to the extremely significant "Urquell," meaning with perfect aptness "original source"—and "source" not only in some abstract sense, but also in the same connotation as our own use of the word as the source of a river or stream. Some further confirmation of this suggestion is given by

[6] In England learner-drivers are obliged
to carry a plate with a large "L."

Mr. Amis (in a personal communication to the writer of this paper, August 1st, 1963) that during the early stages of writing *Lucky Jim* he frequently drank Pilsener Urquell Lager.[7] Quelle is, moreover, a word closely associated with gospel scholarship—as the proto-gospel "Q," beyond which Amis evidently sees a true original gospel, the Ur-Q. (We must reject Dr. Conrad's fanciful suggestion of a connection with the biblical city of Ur.) The omission of the "ell" syllable is in accord with the habit we have already noticed with regard to Margaret, though on this occasion it is naturally practised in discrimination against the words of evil.

It is perhaps true that the highest criticism relates the discoveries made by careful reading, analysis, and meditation to the higher generalities of tradition and ethics. Yet it will be admitted that the basis of such syntheses is the discoveries made in the text. While it would not be difficult to go on from what I have said to a general placing of Amis within the frame of the transcendental tradition which constitutes the major stream of our literature, I feel it more appropriate for the time being to confine myself to the more modest enterprise of representing the facts as they emerge from the text. These are so clear, so consistent, and each detail so obviously fits in with and reinforces the others, that I hardly imagine that my general conclusions are likely to be faulted. But individual points may, of course, be wrong or subject to alternative explanations. If this essay, a first tentative exploration, leads to fuller and more definitive work by other qualified critics, I shall be well content.

For this discussion is not presented as more than a partial note, a first treatment of a theme which has been "strangely neglected" (as Dixon himself comments of his own Word). At this stage it would not have been proper to attempt anything like a definitive analysis. It is hoped, however, that the suggestions put forward will be of service

[7] (At a time when it was obtainable in England under that name. It is, of course, its Czech provenance which purges the coarseness Amis has established as the "colour" characteristic of German language derivatives.)

to further researchers. The fuller investigation which must
follow into the themes of one level of this one book alone,
should give employment for some years to a sufficiency of
trained experts. It is true that modern English literature
presents an almost limitless array of fields of investigation
of this nature. The writer hopes he will be forgiven if he
feels that the theme here treated should receive a certain
priority amongst them, as being more significant than many
that have already been given attention.

—Robert Conquest

A. A. Milne's Honey-Balloon-Pit-Gun-Tail-Bathtubcomplex

By
Karl Anschauung, M.D.

∽ There is often heard the opinion that psychoanalysis is unfriendly to literature, that we regard the artist as a neurotic, that writing is a for us quite antithetical to the Reality Principle activity. What is uncanny [*unheimlich*][1] is that I have often felt this to be true myself. Uncanny I nevertheless say, inasmuch as we who have remained faithful to Freud realize consciously that he was always friendly to art. In his writings find we, it is true, various opinions at various stages of his progress toward a unified field theory of the arts; but although he died untimely before this ultimate together-gathering could be expressed for us, we can see its main outlines sufficiently well to understand the progressive trend of thought which he from the beginning was on. We can now affirm, that at no time did Freud mean seriously to imply that the artist was from other men fully divided by his away-turning from the Reality Principle. True, the artist must be regarded as a Narcissist regrettably unable to overcome regressive ten-

[1] I have reproduced the original German wherever there has been any doubt about shadings of meaning.—Trans.

dencies fixating his libido at pre-Oedipal cathexes, and
hence [also] seeking in masturbatory phantasy-play an
outletting of repressed materials which he upon the unsus-
pecting public wishes to impose in the secondarily elaborated
form of "art." So much, no one would now deny. But as
Freud gathered ever more weighty evidence from his studies,
he gradually realized, that such aetiology not solely to
artists, but to everyone applied—doctor, lawyer, Indian
chief—and that the artist was, if anything, better off than,
let us say, the statesman who, as a result of persisting interest
in infantile theories of anal birth, must send flights of bomb-
ers over other countries and keep himself unusually clean
and fastidious. As for my uncanny feeling that Freud deni-
grated art, in self-analysis I have repressed materials discovered, suggesting this to be a residue of unresolved envy
of the Master dating from our first meeting in 1906 when
I upon the floor passed out cold.

   False then it is, to assert, that Freud with anything but
sincerest respect regarded artists and writers. He was always
quite clear on the point, that the artist *as artist* [*als
Künstler*] was not especially neurotic, was indeed directly
prevented by his art from being as neurotic as the normal
man on the street. For the demands which the Reality
Principle makes upon all of us, no one is entirely prepared;
lucky then is he who a Pleasure Principle outlet can find,
which re-attaches him to reality by earning him honor,
power, riches, fame, and the love of women. Precisely such
a case is the present patient, A. A. Milne. Of neurotic
features in his social character he has displayed little signs,
beyond to be sure the customary psychopathology of every-
day life. For this reason the tireless researcher is encouraged
to out-seek in his art, those perversions, phobias, incipient
psychoses, fixations, sublimations, phantasies, and phyloge-
netic traces, which would have formed his character had he
taken up some other line of work. It is an ontological problem, and not one for our strictly scientific studies, to decide
whether such information, taken together, may be called the
A. A. Milne's-character or must be relegated to the realm of

might-have-been. For my part, I am to the former view inclined, by recalling that no such scruples prevented Jones from explaining Shakespeare's incestuous designs on his mother, nor Ferenczi from discovering Swift's impotence-anxiety-determined distaste for very large girls, nor the Master himself from revealing Leonardo's early relations with a vulture.

Foremost among the problems offered us by *Winnie-the-Pooh* and *The House at the Corner of Pooh's* [*Das Haus bei der Poohecke*], we may place the question, what is Milne's unconscious attitude to bears? The frequent presence on the illusionistic phantasy-screen, or "plot," of these two books, of a bear, strongly points to an obsessive nosology, the which, in fact, is fully in an examination of Milne's poetry borne out. Examine if you please a poem written in early childhood (hence the volume's title *As We Extremely Young Were*), "Lines and Squares":

> *Whenever I walk in a London street,*
> *I'm ever so careful to watch my feet;*
>> *And I keep in the squares,*
>> *And the masses of bears,*
> *Who wait at the corners all ready to eat*
> *The sillies who read on the lines of the street,*
>> *Go back to their lairs,*
>> *And I say to them, "Bears,*
> *Just look how I'm walking in all of the squares!"*[usw.]

Here have we a classic infantile phobia not dissimilar to that of the by-Freud-treated little Hans. Milne imagines that he is on all sides endangered by dreadful bears who will, unless he performs an obsessive ritual essentially similar to those of the Christian Church, attack and devour him. That the suckling babe A. A. Milne found it impossible, to off-shake his phobia in the immediately-following years, we demonstrate with these written at age six:

> Round *about*
> *And* round *about*
> *And* round *about I go;*
> *I think I am a Traveller escaping from a Bear.*

From these early phantasies we draw the plain connection, that *Winnie-the-Pooh* from a defensive reaction mechanism stems, employing the projective technique of inversion of affect: the feared bear becomes the loved bear, the enemy becomes the inseparable-friend. Thus in daydream that severely phobic A. A. Milne makes a pathetic, clinically most interesting attempt, discovered by me, to deny his phobia and rid himself of his obsessive-traits. This diagnosis, as well as explaining the anxiety reduction function of many chapters in the Milne's book,[2] offers a general clue to further psycho-literary mysteries, as will below be seen.

Having shown that the phantasy-character, "Pooh," serves A. A. Milne the purpose, of his bear phobia temporarily to assuage by demanding an affectionate not a libido-inhibited anxiety-response, there remains us the more difficult task to discover what sequence of experiences led the infant A. A. Milne, to his bear phobia in the first place develop. Although Milne's "literary" work is for the purpose to *deny* his phobia intended, we may expect, that under the universal law of the return of the repressed, his repressed materials will of necessity themselves express [*sich aussprechen*] within the text. Of this our expectation the fulfillment is indeed speedy. Before we have even properly at the beginning of the story arrived, find we, in Milne's "Introduction," this note:

> So when Christopher Robin goes to the Zoo, he goes to where the Polar Bears are, and he whispers something to the third keeper from the left, and doors are unlocked, and we wander through dark passages and up steep stairs, until at last we come to the special cage, and the cage is opened, and out trots something brown and furry, and with a happy cry of "Oh, Bear!" Christopher Robin rushes into its arms.

[2] For example: the second poetic fragment above leads us to expect, that somewhere in *Winnie-the-Pooh* an episode will find itself, wherein A. A. Milne placidly stationary remains, while the feared but now fearful bear wanders around and around in a state of uncathected anxiety. Chapter Three, "In Which a Woozle Is by Hunting Pooh and Piglet Nearly Caught," is this case exactly.

Here have we, not merely a confirmation of the overcarry from Milne's poetically celebrated bear-phobia to his bear-character Pooh, but also an unmistakable representation of the underlying Pooh's meaning [*Urpoohdeutung*]. Freud's *Interpretation of Dreams*[3] shows us unequivocally, that to "wander through dark passages and up steep stairs" can only a coitus-equivalent signify. When further we arrive at the opening of a special cage and the out-trotting of something brown and furry, embraced by A. A. Milne, the reader may easily imagine, that all doubt ceases to retain validity. The friendly male bear Pooh is meant, the unfriendly terrifying female organ to represent.

It thus seems likely, that what, the which we have to deal with here, is a Primal Scene[4] witnessed by the infant A. A. Milne, overcharged with free-floating anxiety, and hence into the somewhat more manageable bear-phobia transposed, leading to formation of obsessive ritual meant to avoid to face situations calling for resurgence from the unconscious, past the doors of the preconscious, into the superego-dominated conscious mind of A. A. Milne's, of the repressed material. Thus much is perfectly obvious. There gives no reason to doubt, that all the classic Primal-Scene reactions were in this case present: the sadistic, and secondarily masochistic, misunderstanding of the Scene in terms of assault and battery, the hatred of the father as unique possessor of "Pooh Bear," generalized envy and impotence-anxiety resulting from small size of oneself, resentment of "unfaithful" mother, fear of abandonment, vicarious stimulation of racial memory-traces, and, of course, total repression and "forgetting" of the entire scene. (No piece of evidence is stronger, than the fact, that A. A. Milne never mentions this trauma to anyone.)[5] To critics whose interest is more

[3] Translated by Braille.—Trans.
[4] Students will want to know the exact meaning of this term. A Primal Scene, as I understand it, is an event of great significance (according to the school of thought represented by this article) in the lives of some unlucky small children, who, because of cramped housing conditions, lower-class family habits, or mere chance, find themselves present during functions unsuitable for the healthy development of their imaginations.
[5] I have written him several letters and no reply received.

strictly literary, and not psycholiterary, I leave the work of to document these facts. More pressing in concern for us is the humanitarian task of trying to help A. A. Milne, his bear-phobia to overcome. This will require further and closer attention to a variety of superficially unconnected, actually quite strictly determined and related, elsewhere in the text symptoms.

Let us then upon a seemingly different investigation out-set, and try some word-associations on the patient. Even C. G. Jung, before his unfortunate attack of insanity in 1912, got good results from this technique. The present disadvan-tage, of A. A. Milne's absence from my office, will not hamper us if we in mind keep the realization, that works of art are under conditions of relaxed superego censorship written, thus [also] yielding formerly repressed patterns almost as success-fully, as private analytical sessions, lacking however the stimulating incentives of transference and very high fees. In A. A. Milne's "fictional" memoir *Winnie-the-Pooh* find we a complex of key words, the which points clearly to screen memories hiding the Primal Scene and us helping to exactly the sequence of infantile-experiences reconstruct.

Remembering that A. A. Milne has already been over-excitable proven by references to *pudendum mulieris,* let us propose to him the associations "pit" and "jar," both of course time-honored symbols of the same. To our amazement discover we that these very words are together-joined in the "plot" of *Winnie-the-Pooh.* A. A. Milne explains, in "Piglet a Heffalump Meets," that if he were to attempt, someone to trap, he would do so by employing a jar of honey and a large pit! That "honey" has itself a genital-erotic significance, no one with a good English language command can seriously deny. The inseparability of "Pooh" and honey further cements this identification. Thus have we a cluster, pit-jar-honey, of definite aetiological significance in A. A. Milne's symptom-formation. In this very Heffalump-chapter see we some consequences of this. The Heffalump, whose masculine role so evident is that it was by an ignorant layman noticed,[6] is to fall headlong into the pit-jar-honey "trap"—an exact equivalent, need I hardly say, of the catastrophic Primal Scene effect upon the impressionable tot A. A. Milne. The infantile castration horror, invariable in these cases, breaks past the superego in the thinly-disguised-form of commentary upon honey jars. Thus the jar is a "something mysterious, a shape and no more," and again "a great enormous thing, like—like nothing. A huge big—well, like a—I don't know—like an enormous big nothing." May I point out, that the object inspiring this latter negativistic definition is really Pooh him-or-herself, capped (with redundant symbolism) by a honey jar?

If we now ask A. A. Milne still harder to think about jars, we bring up the following screen memory: the infant A. A. Milne compulsively inserts and removes an ex-balloon from an ex-honey jar, both presented to him by two "others" on his "birthday." Here prove we the hypothesis of racial memory-trace stimulation, for tiny A. A. Milne a dim awareness shows that copulation and childbirth (the birthday) are related. The destructive impression of the Primal Scene is, again, ingeniously by the unconscious represented in terms of burst balloon and emptied jar; while the mechanical, repetitive nature of A. A. Milne's act[7] points to the anxiety neurosis sufferer's obsessive re-enacting of the "others'" (Mummy and Daddy's) traumatic activity, in the hope of this time generating adequate ego-responses to cathect anxiety.

Our list of screen-associations now reads, pit-jar-honey-balloon. At once A. A. Milne the further association recalls, balloon-honey-gun. Upon investigation find we, that in the very first chapter of his most interesting memoir, A. A. Milne himself imagines as flying upward toward honey, aided by a balloon, and shot down by a gun. This is self-explana-

[6] Myron Masterson, "Velenous Happy Land: Pooh's Chassis."

[7] This is not of course the only repetition-compulsion example in *Winnie-the-Pooh*, a book in which the Nirvana principle and the sadomasochistic complex also lavishly illustrated are. The force of Thanatos, perhaps nowhere better illustrated is, than in A. A. Milne's neurotic chanting, "Cottleston, Cottleston, Cottleston Pie," a bearing much further analysis hum.

tory. On the wings of male potency—symbolized by the expanded balloon which characteristically "deflated" was by the Primal Scene—A. A. Milne hopes with infantile naïveté, the previously explained honey to seize. Instead he is discouraged and punished, by the agency of a gun, evidently representing the superior paternal phallus. It is now clear, that the A. A. Milne's-bear-phobia upon a solid base of impotence-anxiety resides. This is confirmed by the next association of "gun." "Coming to see me have my bath?" A. A. Milne recalls having asked his father immediately after the shooting, and when the father somewhat ambiguously answered, young Milne this question added: "I didn't hurt him when I shot him, did I?" The projection of himself into the maiming-father's-role here, altogether predictable was as a typical defense; much more interesting [*interessanter*] is the introduction of a new, exhibitionistic element in the neurosis. Having himself hallucinated into the personage of castrating imago, young Milne "worries" about the over-efficiency of his organ in its intimidation of the father. He wants the father him to watch bathing, ostensibly for the purpose to reassure him that he (A. A. Milne) is still child-like. Yet at the same time, the experienced analyst cannot himself prevent, from seeing a more ego-syntonic motivation here. The screen-memory of being watched bathing by the father, surely a superego-distortion is, for *watching the father bathing,* the which in turn is, perfectly obviously, desired for the reason of reassuring oneself that the father really lacking is, in the terrifying physical power observed in the Primal Scene. A superficial and benevolent exhibitionism, in other words, a secondary elaboration for a malicious skoptophilia[8] is.

Skoptophilia, as the Master has taught us, is proper to the pre-genital organization of the libido, and specifically, to the anal-sadistic phase. Recalling the slang meaning of "Pooh," we see that the suckling A. A. Milne a further problem had—as yet unresolved—confusing anal theories of childbirth with his memory of the Primal Scene. With this

[8] This word is not in my dictionary.—Ed.

clue seek we among Milne's recollections a series of references
to the erogenous zone in question. At once the final piece
in our little puzzle, to us itself presents. A certain ass, A. A.
Milne recalls, has *lost its tail.* The meaning of this missing
object is never in doubt. Its owner extremely "attached to
it" was; "it reminds me of something," says A. A. Milne;
and "somebody must have taken it," adds he, echoing every
child's feeling upon stumbling across the between boys
and girls difference. Upon the re-attachment of this object,
A. A. Milne so affected is, that he "came over all funny,
and had to hurry home for a little snack of something to
sustain him." Now, this rather complicated phantasy shows
us, that A. A. Milne still unconsciously some doubt retains,
as to the basic mechanical principles operative in the Primal
Scene. Whether intercourse is posterior or anterior, he evidently cannot decide. Hence in his phantasy of helpful restoration to the "wounded" mother, he to the mistaken side
wishes to re-attach the "tail." His motive for so doing is
divided, between (1) wish to ingratiate oneself with mother
by doing useful errand, (2) provide weapon (along lines of
sadistic misinterpretation of Scene) for mother to counter-
attack and possibly slay father, (3) demonstrate one's own
ability to serve family harmony by skillful manipulation
of "tail," quite improbable in reality, and (4) general tendency
of small children not their own business to be able to mind.
That A. A. Milne himself imagines, upon completion of this
feat, a snack of honey proceeding to devour, uncovers his
absolutely basic, underlying all else motive in this projection,
namely a most encouraging, perfectly healthy and normal
Oedipal plan, his mother to seduce.

This last feature leads us to believe, that A. A. Milne, if
he will present himself for treatment, an excellent chance
stands of becoming out-straightened. His case is a relatively
simple one of advanced animal-phobia and obsessional defense, somewhat complicated it is true by anal-sadistic and
oral-helpful phantasies, skoptophilia and secondary exhibitionism, latently homosexual trends in identification with
the mother, severe castration anxiety and compensatory

assertiveness, and persistence of infantile misconstructions of birth, intercourse, and excretion. Doubtless when he appears in my office A. A. Milne further little symptoms will reveal, such as nail-biting, fascination with the analyst's foot, excessive squabbling over fees, and so on [*und so weiter*]. All these, Herr Milne, and others may to the surface be brought, and you may, as you in all likelihood wished to be in undertaking your confessions to write, become a healthy and useful member-of-society. Whatever therapeutic value you have achieved from your dirty linen before the general public airing, think how much more you will get from it presenting in a bundle to me. My deductive powers, plus your limitless ability, obscene and meaningful phantasies to regurgitate, might combine, many hundreds of happy and fruitful analytic hours to create for us both.

—Frederick C. Crews

Scholarshipship

>>>>>>>>>>>>>>>>>>>>>

Shakespeare Explained

Pericles

Act II. Scene 3

Enter First Lady-in-Waiting (Flourish,[1] Hautboys[2] and[3] torches[4]).

First Lady-in-Waiting—What[5] ho![6] Where[7] is[8] the[9] music?[10]

Notes

1. *Flourish:* The stage direction here is obscure. Clarke claims it should read "flarish," thus changing the meaning of the passage to "flarish" (that is, the King's), but most authorities have agreed that it should remain "flourish," supplying the predicate which is to be flourished. There was at this time a custom in the countryside of England to flourish a mop as a signal to the passing vendor of berries, signifying that in that particular household there was a consumer-demand for berries, and this may have been meant in this instance. That Shakespeare was cognizant of this custom of flourishing the mop for berries is shown in a similar passage in the second part of King Henry IV, where he has the Third Page enter and say, "Flourish." Cf. also Hamlet, IV, 7: 4.

2. *Hautboys*, from the French *haut*, meaning "high" and the Eng. *boys*, meaning "boys." The word here is doubtless used in the sense of "high boys," indicating either that

Shakespeare intended to convey the idea of spiritual distress
on the part of the First Lady-in-Waiting or that he did not.
Of this Rolfe says: "Here we have one of the chief indica-
tions of Shakespeare's knowledge of human nature, his
remarkable insight into the petty foibles of this work-a-day
world." Cf. T. N. 4: 6, "Mine eye hath play'd the painter,
and hath stell'd thy beauty's form in table of my heart."

3. *and.* A favorite conjunctive of Shakespeare's in referring
to the need for a more adequate navy for England. Tauchnitz
claims that it should be pronounced "und," stressing the
anti-penult. This interpretation, however, has found disfavor
among most commentators because of its limited significance.
We find the same conjunctive in A. W. T. E. W. 6: 7, "Steel-
boned, unyielding *and* uncomplying virtue," and here there
can be no doubt that Shakespeare meant that if the King
should consent to the marriage of his daughter the excuse
of Stephano, offered in Act 2, would carry no weight.

4. *Torches.* The interpolation of some foolish player
and never the work of Shakespeare (Warb.). The critics of
the last century have disputed whether or not this has
been misspelled in the original, and should read "trochies"
or "troches." This might well be since the introduction of
tobacco into England at this time had wrought havoc with
the speaking voices of the players, and we might well imagine
that at the entrance of the First Lady-in-Waiting there
might be perhaps one of the hautboys mentioned in the
preceding passage bearing a box of troches or "trognies"
for the actors to suck. Of this entrance Clarke remarks:
"The noble mixture of spirited firmness and womanly modesty, fine sense and true humility, clear sagacity and absence
of conceit, passionate warmth and sensitive delicacy, generous
love and self-diffidence with which Shakespeare has endowed
the First Lady-in-Waiting renders her in our eyes one of
the most admirable of his female characters." Cf. M. S. N.
D. 8: 9, "That solder'st close impossibilities and mak'st them
kiss."

5. *What*—What.

6. *Ho!* In conjunction with the preceding word doubtless

means "What ho!" changed by Clarke to "What hoo!" In the original MS. it reads "What hi!" but this has been accredited to the tendency of the time to write "What hi" when "what ho" was meant. Techner alone maintains that it should read "What humpf!" Cf. Ham. 5: 0, "High-ho!"

7. *Where.* The reading of the folio, retained by Johnson, the Cambridge editors and others, but it is not impossible that Shakespeare wrote "why," as Pope and others give it. This would make the passage read "Why the music?" instead of "Where is the music?" and would be a much more probable interpretation in view of the music of that time. Cf. George Ade. Fable No. 15, "Why the gunnysack?"

8. *is*—is not. That is, would not be.

9. *the.* Cf. Ham. 4: 6. M. S. N. D. 3: 5. A. W. T. E. W. 2: 6. T. N. 1: 3 and Macbeth 3: 1, "that knits up *the* raveled sleeves of care."

10. *music.* Explained by Malone as "the art of making music" or "music that is made." If it has but one of these meanings we are inclined to think it is the first; and this seems to be favored by what precedes, "*the* music!" Cf. M. of V. 4: 2, "The man that hath no music in himself."

The meaning of the whole passage seems to be that the First Lady-in-Waiting has entered concomitant with a flourish, hautboys and torches and says, "What ho! Where is the music?"

—Robert Benchley

An Imaginary Review

"Prolegomena for a System of Intuitive Reasoning." By
*F. W. Wiertz. Translated from the third German edition by
Julia Elson. (The Channer-Webb Co., New York).*

〜 It speaks ill for the enterprise of our publishing firms
that it should have been left to an American firm to bring
out the first English translation of Friedrich Wiertz's *magnum
opus.* It was as long ago as 1894 that the late David An-
drews—a man who, owing possibly to his lack of an academic
connection, never won the philosophic reputation that was
his due—first drew the attention of English students to
Wiertz by his excellent rendering of the "Torso of Apollo."
Since then the remainder of Wiertz's *Aesthetic* has also
been translated, although remarkably badly. But the theory
of æsthetics was to him little more than a side show. He
threw great light on some most obscure problems. Unlike
many philosophers who have written on the subject, he had
some appreciation of beauty; and there are passages in the
"Torso" which, from the general reader's point of view, are
as amusing, as well-written and at least as sane as the best
critical and polemic passages of Nietzsche in his anti-Wagner
period. Nevertheless, Wiertz himself attached small importance to these works, and his chief interest lay elsewhere.
He believed, and he believed rightly, that there was more
permanent value in the "Prolegomena" than in all his other
writings put together; and it seems preposterous that we
should have had to wait until he has been in the grave ten
years, before getting an English version of a book which
will continue to mould European thought when most of
his contemporaries are forgotten. It is characteristic of this

country. Wiertz is ignored and they bombard us with Eucken.

The first sentence of the book is an earnest of what follows. "When doctors disagree," says Wiertz, "honest men come by their own"; combining two proverbs which exist both in German and in English. There follows a rapid but most brilliant sketch of the history of philosophy from Heraclitus and Pythagoras to Hoffding, Herbert Spencer and T. H. Green, in whom he seems to have taken a special delight. Briefly analysing their systems, or the systems that have been foisted on them by their followers, he shows that almost all of them have been subject to primary delusions that have vitiated the whole of their work. They have made assumptions that they have comfortably stowed out of sight when they thought the reader was not looking. They have drugged themselves into a belief in the all-potency of logic and of analysis. They have been mastered by their own metaphors. They have allowed themselves to think that what cannot be solved in any other way can be solved by a manipulation of words. They have "built long thin ladders into the air, some with many rungs, but all no more capable of containing, or, rather, of comprehending, the universe than my hair is of comprehending the atmosphere." With delightful wit he demolishes "the ancient, modern, and mediæval scholastic philosophies." He quotes Rubinoff: "The philosophers of all sects have spent three thousand years burying the fair form of Truth under a mass of verbal sewage." This unsavoury accumulation Wiertz, with a grace that leads one to suspect him of non-Teuton blood, shovels aside with great sweeps of the pen and drops on the benighted heads of its original depositors.

"Down with Words," "Down with Philosophers," "Down with Systems"; these are three of his next chapter headings. The uninitiated might well wonder why he proceeded to imitate those whom he denounced. The reader has taken respectfully his descriptions of his predecessors: Plato, "a bad artist with a depraved taste for social reform"; Hegel, "a windbag who was born burst"; Schopenhauer, "a dyspeptic mushroom on half-pay"; Spinoza, "a wandering Jew"; Kant, "a corpulent cypher"; Zeno, "a lamp-post without a lamp"; Fichte, "the echo of a bad smell"; Aristotle, "an industrious publisher's hack," and so on. What had he to do with words and systems? How did he hope to escape the lot of all the others who have attempted to "draw maps of the dark side of the moon"? It is bare justice to him to say that he realised the inconsistency; it is also bare justice to add that he never constructed a system, though he had the temerity to provide materials for a system that a more foolish successor might construct. But, still he did not confine himself to destructive criticism, to negation. He was not a philosopher of the study. He had had a training in positive science, and for some time he even took part in the politics of Saxony, his state. Never losing sight of his limitations, he achieved by experiment and speculation results which, whatever their relation to the Eternal Sphinx, may be of the greatest practical value.

It is impossible here to detail the way in which Wiertz arrived at his method, or the manner in which he, with unexampled lucidity, defended its use. Roughly speaking, his process was this: "What," he asked, "is the usual concept of a concept?" After examining and rejecting a number of illustrations for it he chose that of the unfolding mirror that is being continually breathed upon. By induction he concluded that if the breath could be removed the mirror would become clearer. Both experience and common-sense (which, though he could not defend it, he deemed important) tell us that the operation of stopping the breath cannot be performed by a phenomenal agency. We have to look, then (and even Hegel could not have rejected this conclusion), for a non-phenomenal, or, rather, a super-phenomenal agency. But this super-phenomenal agency can only be grasped by super-phenomenal means; and here Wiertz's years in the laboratories came to his rescue. He had noticed, when weighing sections of an amoeba, that the weight of the sections was always less than that of the whole, and that the discrepancy varied with the temperature, being greatest when the temperature was high and least when it was low. For this Residuum, to which he chose to give the name Supraliminal Intuition, he discovered the formula: Cos 65 log $2 = 23 \sin 45 + \sqrt{2^{15}}$. On this formula which can convey but little to anyone who is not a mathematician, he built, by a long and careful process of argument, his theory or, rather, his working hypothesis of the Intuitive Reason. It is this process that fills the greater part of the "Prolegomena." To the average reader these chapters must of necessity be difficult and rather dull. But it is well worth while making the effort to master them in view of the bearing that they have on the concluding chapter, the chapter that is being made the basis of a whole political theory in Germany and Italy and that some of the French Syndicalists have appropriated to their own use.

The Wiertzians have gone to the most extreme lengths in the affirmations they have made with the "Prolegomena" as justification. When one says this one does not imply that they advocate or assert much that is shocking to bourgeois sentiment in the sense that Nietzsche, Stirner, Marinetti, and Tolstoi are shocking. Where they run to excess is in the meticulousness with which they apply the Wiertzian instrument. Hirsch-Menkendorff, the latest of them, gravely informs the world not merely that women's suffrage is bad, that beer is good, that the government should be run by commercial men, that Sabbatarianism and cruelty to animals go hand in hand, but announces with all the air of a solemn prophet: "God objects to compulsory insurance." Wiertz never went into such detail as this himself. But it may at least be said that there is little that the average middle-class man says or does or thinks that he cannot find defended and justified in his pages. "I am," said he, "the Apotheosis of the Ordinary." It is absurd that he should not have been translated into English before.

Miss Elson's rendering is scholarly and her language clear and idiomatic. But here and there, unfortunately, there are Americanisms that a British audience will scarcely stomach. English people do not allude to a "bunch of philosophers," and for "hand-grip," on page 164, "portmanteau" or "hand-bag" might have been substituted.

—J. C. Squire

Notes and Comments

The Arthurian Creep Mouse Manuscript
by Timothy Trivia, Yeal University

ᕦ The present state of scholarship in medieval studies is far from perfect. What is most disturbing perhaps to those of us who still feel that precision and accuracy are virtues not to be wholly ignored is the neglect that is being shown in some circles for textual, philological, and bibliographical studies. This present paper is a small, but not insignificant attempt to arrest this dangerous movement away from the kind of scholarship which has produced—not that the reader needs any reminder—the only lasting contributions in this century to medieval studies. In the present form in which the paper is now being submitted, tne reader, if he is at all familiar with medieval literaturᴠ, will be perceptive enough to detect that my material is only *superficially* unrelated.

To begin then. The ninth stanza of Ballad #271 in Child's anthology—and, if one finds it more convenient to consult Percy's *Reliques*, #103 in that venerable collection—involves a challenging problem in chronology. The whole difficulty can be resolved, as it will now be demonstrated, if we interpret the crucial phrase, "hast him take and slawe" (line 4276) as an example of the predictive past tense, a tense somewhat reminiscent of the well-known Hebrew prophetic perfect tense, which expresses a future event as if it had occurred in the past. There is no difficulty in finding historical precedents for this use of the predictive past tense if we examine Alfred's translation of Gregory's *Cura Pastoralis, The Blickling Homilies,* Snorri's *Prose Edda,* and several Celtic legends dealing with primitive Arthurian material, which, unfortunately, have been lost.

The mention of Arthurian materials brings us to the next section of the present paper. An anomaly for all students of *Gawain and the Green Knight* has been the interpretation of the word "barlay" in line 3246. In their notes to what sometimes passes for the definitive edition of the poem, Professors Tolkien and Gordon are, as usual, of little help to us here. Relying on evidence presented in an article in *Medium Aevum* by Ellesmere Pearl—an article which is, we suspect, a brilliant piece of scholarship—the present paper brings to light the hitherto undiscovered fact that in the west of England the word "barlay" was used as a shout of triumph in the children's game of creepmouse.[1] It is this meaning, surely, which was intended by the author, for it explains the context more satisfactorily than any meaning previously suggested by scholars, and which results in our finally understanding one of the more significant problems of the poem.

To develop the major point of this paper in another direction, let us turn to the English version of the *Roman de la Rose.* A sustained period of study devoted to the manuscripts of the English translation has led this scholar to conclude that it is not the work of Chaucer (as is thought) but rather a revision by an anonymous North Midland monastic scribe of a translation by a certain as yet unidentified minor figure in the Lydgate tradition. The scribe, whoever he was, was apparently working from memory; he recalled perfectly the first 1700 lines of the original translation, but at this point, perhaps because of some prolonged

[1] By establishing the presence of the now famous "Welsh L" in the pronunciation of "barlay" Professor A. E. Diphthong has, with his usual brilliance, restored at long last the proper number of elements in the alliterative series of line 3246. Copies of Professor Diphthong's paper on this and similar problems in Fourteenth Century pronunciation may be obtained by writing to Professor Diphthong at the Anglo-Frisian Institute of Brightening, Lindisfarne, Northumbria.

outside disturbance—Wars of the Roses, one might suggest[2]—was interrupted from his work, for he mutilated the next 4100 lines of the original, and introduced Northernisms into the text as well. In order to demonstrate the soundness of this thesis, the results of having collated the entire *corpus* of manuscripts—seventy-three in all—will now be presented. Bodleian MS 354, line 3715 corresponds to Digby MS 286, line 1978. The recently reconstructed Rawlinson MS 274, collates well with Harley 2253, *but only up to line 3414;* from here on it seems to follow more closely Ashmolean MS 103 (this would explain why the French word "boutons" is translated up to line 2414 by the word "knoppes" but after line 3414 is rendered into English simply as "buttons."[3]) Bodleian MS 67 (notorious for its scribal errors) also collates well with Harley 3364, but since the exact relationship between these two manuscripts has been a perennial source of spirited, if not bitter, controversy, this writer is at present examining once more the seventy-three manuscripts.

[2] Cf. *Annales Rerum Danicarum Esromenses* (ed. J. Langbek, 1875); Non post multum vero temporis animosus ad uxoris exhortationem Hiarward *Sialandism* classe peciit. Genero suo Rollum tributum attulisse simulavit. Die, quadam dilusente ad Laithram misit, ut videret tributum, Rollum nunciavit (p. 834). (Comment on this passage is surely superfluous.)

[3] A striking parallel to this can be found in Aelfric's *Lives of the Saints* (Text of Kluge's *Angelsachsisches Lesebuch,* 4th edition, 1915, pp. 87–88): Nu raede we on bocum, thaet man araerde haethenyld on callum tham fyrste aer Noes flode, oth thaet tha entas worhton thone wundorlican stypel aefter Noes flode and him swa faela yereorda god thaer foryeaf, swa thaera wyrhtena waes. (We have found it necessary to transcribe into modern type, as is obvious to the reader who is well acquainted with Old English texts.)

Milton Processed—a Review of Recent Process by Snog H. Flatch (Horvard)

Statistics has provided modest if substantial gains in offering solid underpinnings for the notoriously unstable judgments of critics and scholars alike.

As evidence of this heartening progress we have Lompock's derivational analysis of terminal moraines in Longfellow Gorkin's study (Horvard Press) of sutures in the anapestic drinking songs of Thomas Tickell (Pinceton) and, most recently, Professor Throtwell Bull's major examination of mass nouns, count nouns, plus junctures, double bar junctures, terminal tagmemes, medial gramemes, sutures, *pari passu*, feminine endings, masculine pauses, run-ons, and off-prints in Milton (Syraccuse).

Tho I have serious reservations about Bull's work, he undoubtedly has been handicapped by the lack of such resources (pattern playbacks and visual sonographs) as are possessed by the larger universities of the East. Nevertheless, his work—and that of the newly-founded Institute of Statistico-Linguistico-Analysis at Syraccuse—is a step, however modest, in the right direction, and deserves approval from the scholarly world.

But for all his painstaking efforts Bull is seriously in error. While we agree with his conclusion that the traditional dates for Milton's poems are correct, his analysis of the titles of Milton's poems must not go unchallenged.[1]

Bull argues that *Paradise Lost* is *Paradise Lost*. Certainly there would seem to be no dispute here. But Bull merely obfuscates the matter. Bull's figures for the terminal endings of PL (I) and PR (I) are PL: 38.1f and 61.9m, PR: 31.5f and 62.5m. Incomprehensibly, Bull ignores the fact that 1) a given prosodic technique must *increase* in development as it occurs.[2] (He arranges his statistics to fit his argument!)

[1] Bull and myself are in complete agreement that absolute numbers of polysyllables (and even the number per 1000 lines) is not indicative of any major difference in dates or titles.

[2] Hazleman refers to this progress as an obstruct; I prefer the more limited definition.

2) He ignores the true evidence at his very finger-tips—i.e. the close *correspondence* of the two sets of figures, which suggests the close similarity—if not identity—of PL and PR!

My own processing of Milton (thru the 709—Bull's institute is limited only to the 509) indicates that terminal endings occur more frequently at the end of *both* PL and PR, not merely at the end of PL, as Bull would have it.[3]

In other words, *Paradise Lost* is *Paradise Regained*.[4]

Bull's error—and we hope future scholars will not be similarly tempted by the 509—lies in the ignoring of *suggestive* statistics. The correspondences here are not identical—but they are *suggestive*.

The importance of such statistical proof, only to Milton's titles, biography, criticism, and the full appreciation of his poetic achievements is, I believe, manifest.[5]

A Scandalously Misdated Wordsworth Letter
By Delver Tryffya
(Cornwall Normal College)

Wordsworth's letter to the Bishop of Llandaffy, which Annette Vallon dated Rydal Mount, 14 Sept., 1816, should obviously be dated Daffdyllyclydd, 15 Sept., 1798. Daffdyllyclydd was where Wordsworth stopped briefly while on his walking trip from Yorkshire to visit Coleridge in Cumberland. The new dating makes clear beyond any possible doubt that Wordsworth slept at the soon-to-be-immortalized White Doe Inn on the night of 15 Sept., 1798.

[3] The conclusion which looms from my own processing suggests that there is also a noticeable shift in pauses, in both PR and PL—not merely PL. See my article, "Strong Pauses in the First Half, the Exact Middle, and the Second Half of the Line," *Journal of Water Imagery*, XIV (1958), 651–701.

[4] Hughes, Parker, French et al. hold different views on this matter.

[5] See my forthcoming book, *The Title Regained: Pyrrhic Endings in Milton*.

Hardy's Reputation as Poet: A Modern Satire of Circumstance

Grigori G. Grimstone
(Coalbin College, Maine)

It is not enough that we recognize the essentially comic apperceptions manifest in Hardy's poetry. The complex situational aspects of his *Satires of Circumstance* and *Life's Little Ironies* have all too often been carelessly dismissed—ironically enough—as "confused" and "inconsequential" by American critics, and almost thoroughly ignored by British critics, who—ironically enough—have failed utterly to grasp fully these manifestations of Hardy's unique genius for the comic ironic, these manifestations which reflect so sharply and so accurately both the reality and the actuality of Hardy's moulding-place, the Wessex he loved so well and the era he as thoroughly detested. They fail, that is, to see precisely how Hardy's genius came to grips with the raw material provided by his environment, and transmuted it into everlasting art.

But let us not sell Hardy's vision short. The confusion in the poetry is not his; it is the confusion of his time (and, should I add, of ours?), expressed with complete deliberation and control, and with consummate tragic irony.

Trollope and Marconi: A Necessary Clarification
By S. O. Watt
London Association of Postal Servants
(Formerly London Association of Postal Employees), Bristol Branch

The Marconi mentioned in the minutes of the Philosophical Association, London, as having read from a manuscript
of his at the meeting of June 31, 1867, was undoubtedly
Guglielmo Niccolo Marconi, Corresponding Secretary of
the London Association of Postal Employees, and not
Guglielmo Giovanni Marconi the Italian poet. Trollope
read some recommendations at this meeting for the improve-
ment of the pillar box (which he had invented). (It should
be here mentioned also that neither was this the Guglielmo
Marconi who was later to invent the wireless; he was not
born till 1874.) Guglielmo Giovanni Marconi, whom writers
on Trollope generally assume to have been the Marconi
mentioned in the minutes, could not have delivered the
above mentioned address, for Trollope was to write in a
letter of August 2, 1867 that he had not yet met the poet,
*but was, indeed, looking forward to doing so upon his
forthcoming arrival in London from Thomas Adolphus
Trollope's villa in Naples.*

A Fitzgerald Crux Uncrossed
By Klaus D. Ogen
(Western Kansas College of
Optometric Science)

One of the more puzzling critical cruces of Fitzgerald scholarship during recent years has been the problem of Fitzgerald's inspiration for that key symbol of *The Great Gatsby,* that puzzling, omnivideotic representation of the Deity—the Eyes of Dr. T. J. Eckleburg. The light-casting document is a bill from Fitzgerald's optometrist, Dr. James Gatz. The bill is dated February 3, 1923, and requests payment of $55.00 "For Services Rendered." Its apparently mundane nature might at first lead the casual scholar to overlook its true significance, yet significant it is. We know for a fact that "the Eyes of Dr. T. J. Eckleburg" did not appear in the original version of the novel. Whence then *did* they derive? I think we have now not far to look. The cogent data are these:

  a. The bill bears a date of Feb. 3, 1923, at which time Fitzgerald was certainly revising the MS of *Gatsby,* and

  b. The printed letterhead at the top of the artifact gives not only the doctor's name, address and telephone number, but also includes *a large pair of spectacles,* a reproduction of the advertising sign which—apparently—hung over Dr. Gatz's dispensary.

Though the traditional academician may scoff at the non-ostentatious and the humble, the truly conscientious scholar does not neglect evidence which stares him in the face.

Overlooked Epic Element in Fielding's Tom Jones or *Another Epic Parallel in Fielding's* Tom Jones

By Robert Devereaux Lee
(*University of Northwest Carolina*)

Any careful perusal of "the greatest English novel" (Baker, *History of the English Novel, Supp.,* 1939, p. 361) reveals a number of close parallels with the great epic literature of the classical past. Many of the more significant parallels are, as all of us well know, between the eponymous protagonist of Vergil's *Aeneid* and the eponymous hero of Fielding's masterpiece. But the very abundance of such similarities has led, paradoxically, to a critical dilemma. While the offspring of Vergil's hero are credited with the founding of Great Rome and Mighty Britain, *Fielding's hero has no offspring at the conclusion of the massive novel;* we cannot even project such a post-novel development without treading upon extremely thin critical ice.

Are we to think, then, that Fielding—whose library attests emphatically to his deep knowledge of the classics—has neglected the obvious in erecting his epic structure? I think not. Rather it is we—who egocentrically and perhaps not always with reason call ourselves modern—who have *overlooked* the obvious. Fielding chose the surname of his hero with much care after reading with avidity in *The Tatler* of the recent establishment of the Carolinian city of Jonesboro across the sea in the soon-to-be-lost New World. "Modern" scholars seem sometimes to have forgotten that our nation was once integrally a part of the nation founded by Brut, and in their zeal to put forward favourite theories—or should we say hypotheses—fail to look at their feet for the evidence which puts itself in their way. How the Bow Street Magistrate would have laughed to see his meaning obstructed for more than two centuries!

—*Motley Hands*

The Literary World

>>>>>>>>>>>>>>>>>>>>>>>>>>>>>>>

My Memories of
D. H. Lawrence

 ⮌ If you wander around in bookstores you will have come upon several books about D. H. Lawrence: Mr. John Middleton Murry's autobiography, Frieda Lawrence's memoirs, Keith Winter's *roman à clef* called "Impassioned Pygmies," etc. These are all comparatively recent; a complete bibliography going back to the time of Lawrence's death would run into hundreds of items, maybe thousands. The writing man is pretty much out of it if he hasn't written something about how hard it was to understand, to talk to, and to get along generally with D. H. Lawrence; and I do not propose to be out of it. I had my difficult moments on account of the Master, and I intend to tell about them—if Mr. Murry will quit talking for a moment and let me talk.

I first met D. H. Lawrence on a train platform in Italy twelve years ago. He was pacing up and down. There was no mistaking the reddish, scraggly beard, the dark, beetling eyebrows, the intense, restless eyes. He had the manner of a man who was waiting for something; in this case, I think it was the train. I had always wanted to meet the great artist and here was my golden opportunity. I finally screwed my courage up to the accosting point and I walked over and accosted him. "D. H. Lawrence?" I said. He frowned,

stopped, pulled a watch out of his vest pocket, and held
it up to me so that I could see the dial. "No speak Eyetal-
ian," he said. "Look for yourself." Then he walked away.
It had been about 10:12 or 10:13 A.M. by his watch (I had
10:09 myself, but I may have been slow). Since we both got
on the train that pulled into the station a few minutes
later, I contrived to get into the same compartment with
him and to sit down next to him. I found him quite easy to
talk to. He seemed surprised that I spoke English—on the
platform he had taken me for an Italian who wanted to
know what time it was. It turned out after a few minutes
of rather puzzling conversation that his name was George
R. Hopkins and that he had never heard of D. H. Lawrence.
Hopkins was a resident of Fitchburg, Massachusetts, where
he had a paper factory. He wished to God he was back in
the United States. He was a strong Coolidge man, thought
every French person was depraved, and hadn't been able to
find a decent cup of coffee in all Europe. He had a married
daughter, and two sons in Penn State, and had been having
trouble with a molar in his lower jaw ever since he arrived
in Le Havre, some three weeks before. He wouldn't let
anybody monkey with it, he said, except a certain Dr. Karns
in Fitchburg. Karns was an Elk and a bird-dog fancier in
addition to being the best dentist in the United States.

    This encounter did not discourage me. I determined to
meet D. H. Lawrence before I came back to America, and
eventually I sat down and wrote him a note, asking him
for the opportunity of meeting him (I had found out where
he was living at the time—in Florence, I believe, though I
may be wrong). I explained that I was a great admirer of
his—I addressed him simply as Dear Master—and that I had
some ideas about sex which I thought might interest him.
Lawrence never received the letter, it transpired later, because
I had unfortunately put it in the wrong envelope. He got
instead a rather sharp note which I had written the same
evening to a psychoanalyst in New York who had offered to
analyze me at half his usual price. This analyst had come
across some sketches I had made and had apparently jumped

to the conclusion that it would be interesting to try to get at what was behind them. I had addressed this man in my note simply as "sir" and I had told him that if he wanted to analyze somebody he had better begin with himself, since it was my opinion there was something the matter with him. As for me, I said, there was nothing the matter with me. This, of course, was the letter that Lawrence got, owing to the shifting of envelopes, and I was later to understand why I never heard from Lawrence and also why I kept hearing from the analyst all the time. I hung around Europe for several months waiting for a letter from Lawrence, and finally came home, in a low state of mind.

I eventually met, or rather talked with, D. H. Lawrence about six months after I got back to New York. He telephoned me one evening at my apartment. "Hello," I said into the transmitter. "Hello," a voice said. "Is this Mr. Thurber?" "Yes," I said. "Well, this is D. H. Lawrence," said the voice. I was taken back; for a moment I couldn't say a word, I was so surprised and excited. "Well, well," I said, finally, "I didn't know you were on this side." "This is the right side to be on, isn't it?" he asked, in a rather strained voice (I felt that he was excited, too). "Yes, it is," I said. "Well," said Lawrence, "they turned me over on my right side because my left side hurt me so." Thereupon he began to sing "Frankie and Johnny." He turned out to be a waggish friend of mine who had heard my stories about trying to get in touch with D. H. Lawrence, and was having me on.

I never did get to meet D. H. Lawrence, but this I rarely admit. Whenever I am at a cocktail party of literary people and the subject of Lawrence comes up, I tell my own little anecdote about the Master: how he admired Coolidge, how he had trouble with his teeth, how he liked to sing "Frankie and Johnny." These anecdotes are gaining considerable currency and I have no doubt that they will begin to creep into biographies of the man in a short time. Meanwhile I have become what you could almost call allergic to famous writers. I suppose this is the natural outgrowth of my curious and somewhat disturbing relationship with D. H. Lawrence. I cannot truthfully say that any part of that relationship was satisfactory, and therefore I am trying to forget D. H. Lawrence, which makes me about the only writer in the world who is. It is a distinction of a sort.

—James Thurber

Tiptoeing Down Memory Lane

⤳ In these random wanderings down "Memory Lane" (as I call it—and who does not?) I am relying chiefly on a rather faulty faculty for reminiscence, a diary, belonging to somebody else, for 1890 (or rather the first three weeks of 1890, ending with a big blot) and some old bound volumes of *Harper's Round Table* for 1895–7 (1896 missing). For any discrepancies or downright lies, I beg the indulgence due an old man who has already become something of a bore.

Life in literary circles in New York during the late eighteen-nineties and early eighteen-seventies was quite different from literary life today. In the first place, more authors wore large mustaches and beards, which complicated things considerably. One might meet Walt Whitman (if one weren't careful) and think that it was Joachim Miller, except for the fact that Whitman lived in the East and Miller (thank God!) lived in the West. I remember on one occasion that Miller met Whitman in the lobby of the old Fifth Avenue Hotel (then just the plain Fifth Avenue Hotel, without the "old") and Miller said: "For a minute I thought you were Miller!" to which Whitman replied: "For a minute I thought you were Whitman!" It was a contretemps, all right. And not a very good one, either.

All of this made literary contacts very confusing in the old days, whereas today they are so simple that one may avoid them entirely by not going to teas or reading the book notes. I very well remember my first literary contact when I came to New York as a young boy of sixty-five in 1890. I had been out writing a novel, as all young boys were apt to do in those days, and came in, all hot and excited, to find Bret Harte, Frank Norris, Charles Warren Stoddard, and Irving Caesar waiting for me to talk over Mark Twain's latest story about the Drunken Frog of Calvados County. The last part of it hadn't come over the wire yet, so it didn't make much sense as a funny story, but we all laughed heartily at it because it was afterward to become so famous. I shall never forget Charles Dudley Warner's face as he laughed at it. It was terrible.

It was only a few weeks later that Mark Clemens ("Samuel Twain") asked me to lunch at the Century. I was very busy on my new book, and rather hated to leave off work as I hadn't even found my pencil, but my wife said that she thought that I ought to go as it would make such a nice tidbit for my memoirs later. I had also heard that the Century served a very delicious roast-beef hash, browned to a crisp, which was an added attraction. Sometime I must write a book of literary reminiscences about roast-beef hash browned to a crisp.

So I went. And was I bored! The hash was great, but Edmund Clarence Stedman, Henry Fuller, and Richard Watson Gilder all told the Drunken Frog story, and Mark Clemens ("Samuel Langhorne") acted it out, and what with beards and mustaches and jumpings up and down, I finally begged off and went to the Players' to meet J. I. C. Clark, Hamlin Garland, "Buster" West, and Dr. Johnson (who was not really dead at that time but only "playing possum").

I remember that it was on that day that I was an unwilling auditor to one of the most famous interplays of rapier wit which ever devastated a literary memoir. Nat Goodwin took me around to see a rehearsal of "All's Well That Ends All," where I met Sir Beerbohm Tree, who was in this country straightening out a little libel suit (he had accused William Winter of stealing one of his gags and Winter had retaliated with a suit claiming that the gag was no good anyway). Sir Beerbohm (Tree) was engaged at that moment in a controversy with Lester Wallack, so-named after Wallack's Theatre.

The two wits had been discussing something connected

with the theatre (otherwise they wouldn't have been able to discuss at all) and Sir Beerbohm had said:

"All right, that's what *you* think!"

Wallack looked about him with a quizzical smile.

"Very well," he said, dryly, "if that's the way you feel about it."

Tree threw back his leonine head and glared.

"I see!" he said, and walked away.

It was a big day for repartee.

Early in January of that year (what year?) Walt Whitman confided to me that he was doing a play, to be called "Ten Nights in a Broad-brimmed Hat." I told him that it would never go, as there was no adagio dancer in it. He said that he felt that adagio dancing was going out, and that what the public wanted was something good and sexy without people actually throwing each other about. I never liked Whitman, because of his having once worked on a Brooklyn newspaper, but I told him that the only thing to do was to try it out in Newark and see how it went. I never heard anything more of the play—or of Whitman.

In my diary (or the diary that I am using) I find an entry: "Oct. 12th. This is the end! Filkins has gone too far." I am frankly mystified by this entry. So far as I know, there has been no character in our literary history by the name of Filkins (unless it was Ringold Lardner using another name) and I cannot understand just what bearing he has on this matter. If I had my wits about me, I should never include him in this biography. He means nothing.

It was just about this time that Ralph Waldo Emerson had been dead for ten years, so I never knew him. I did know a man named Emerson Cottner, however, which gives me a pretty good loophole for bringing the Sage of Concord (or was that Thoreau?) into these pages. Although I never knew Waldo Emerson (as we used to call him) I thought that he was all right.

During the fall before we went back to Hyannis to live, we were the center of quite a round of literary activity. I say "quite a round of literary activity." I mean that I went to the Century to a dinner given for William Dean Howells. It was a delightful occasion, and I got many names for my list, as well as two new overcoats. Horace Greeley, Richard Watson Gilder, Robert Underwood Johnson, Horace Watson Gilder, Richard Underwood Johnson, Robert Greeley, Otto H. Kahn, Charles Dudley Warner, Thomas Bailey Aldrich, Mrs. S. Standwood Menken (as *Columbia*). Music by the Yacht Club Boys.

I shall never forget an incident which occurred between Horace Watson Aldrich and Mark Twain ("Samuel Langhorne Gibson") during dinner. Twain got up and announced that owing to the limited capacity of the room, most of the people there would have to eat their dinners up in the Children's Room of the Century (for members under sixty). At this, Aldrich (or Gilder, as we used to call him), proposed a toast to "Our Absent Members," which J. A. B. Fuller, having only one leg, took personally, and stamped out of the room in a rage. It was delicious.

At Maybie's quip, a roar went up (which turned out to be from the furnace downstairs), but a great many of us, including Emily Dickinson (who, I thought, had never left Amherst, Mass., but who seemed to get around quite a bit for a recluse) all joined in the laughter, which was negligible. I shall never forget it, at least, not until this book gets proofread and off the presses. I think that my next book will be more in the nature of a serious history where I won't have to remember so many things.

And so we come to the end of the road. What lies beyond, what literary contacts are to be made, all must remain a mystery. (I might make a mystery story out of it, in fact.) There are so many figures in American life which do not come within the scope of this poor outline. But if I can hurry around and get some invitations, I may be able to add a few more names before the next issue. But by the next issue perhaps all my pretty little readers will have flown away. Frankly, I could hardly blame them.

Sic transit gloria mundi (as we used to call him).

—*Robert Benchley*

The Critics: A Conversation

✑ MR. HUDNUT. Who has read Hornblende's latest?

MR. BIRD. Not I! I looked into it, and the first thing my eye lit upon was a letter purporting to be written by a Frenchman in which the date was given 1 Janvier with a capital J. After that, I really couldn't go on with it!

MR. HUDNUT. Of course, I think Hornblende's cosmopolitan pretensions are among the most amusing things in contemporary literature. He has never been abroad in his life, you know, but he gets someone over there to supply him with a lot of continental theater programs and menus, which he memorizes for purposes of conversation.

MR. BIRD. Really! Ha-ha-ha! Marvellous! Marvellous!

A LADY. Well, this last book of his almost makes one wonder what one could have seen in the others. It's so *dull,* and so *sentimental!*

MR. HUDNUT. Oh, Bert has always been sentimental—the most sentimental man in the world! All this great show of brutality and ruthlessness with which he tries to impress his readers is merely a screen to defend himself against his own emotions. You know, he always sends a valentine every year to the first girl he was ever in love with—out in South Dakota somewhere.

THE LADY. Well, I'm very much interested to hear that, because that's what I have always felt about him—that he was essentially a weak man trying to disguise his weakness by bluster. It's as if he were continually calling a spade a spade just to show he's not afraid to.

MR. LATROBE. And, after all, everything that Hornblende tries to do has already been done so much better by Charles Lavender.

THE LADY. Oh, yes: Charles Lavender!

MR. HUDNUT. Who is Lavender, Latrobe? I've never heard of him.

MR. LATROBE. Charles Lavender was an exquisite artist, though he's hardly known today.

MR. HUDNUT. When did he live?

MR. LATROBE. All his best work came out in the nineties. He treated the sort of subject that Hornblende tries to deal with—and I think it's quite obvious what Hornblende's subjects really are—but gracefully, poignantly, charmingly!

MR. HUDNUT. How can you get hold of Lavender's books?

MR. LATROBE. They're almost impossible to find nowadays. I suppose that I am probably the only person in America who has a complete collection.

MR. HUDNUT. I'd like to borrow them some time.

MR. LATROBE. I'm sorry, but I never lend my books— especially my Lavender firsts.

MR. BIRD. I couldn't resist calling Hornblende's blunder to the attention of Jacques Champfleury!

MR. HUDNUT. Yes—tell us about your controversy with Champfleury. I missed the last *Revue Libre*.

MR. BIRD. Well: to begin at the beginning, in 1895, when the old *Revue de Lutèce* was started, an announcement appeared in the first number to the effect that one of the features of the magazine was to be the cultivation of English literature—with all the usual rot about promoting the inter-change of ideas between the two countries—and in the very next number there appeared an article on the English novel spelling Dickens D-i-k-e-n-s. D-i-k-e-n-s! I ventured at the time to point out this little error to the editors and received a polite but insincere reply from Camille Vide, who had written the article—professing his profoundest regret and explaining that a correction would be published—which in due course appeared, also polite but insincere. Five months later, in another article, this time on a French subject,

Monsieur Vide informed the world that *Le Kiosque Parfumé*
of Tristan Kraus had appeared in 1879. Well: there I had
him on his own ground! The first edition of *Le Kiosque
Parfumé*, limited to twenty-five copies, was privately printed
in 1877—two years earlier than that! I wrote an article
in excellent French which I called *Les Erreurs de M.
Vide* and sent it to the rival magazine, *La Revue de Deux Rives*.
Well: to make a long story short, the *Lutèce* crowd have
never forgiven me. They reviewed my bibliography of the
Mexican drama in the most perfunctory fashion, garbling
the passages they translated—

THE LADY (*talking to Hudnut, while Latrobe listens to
Bird*). I'm so relieved to hear you say that you don't think
Bertram Hornblende is really such a tremendous figure.
That's what I've always felt, but up to this latest book
I've never dared to admit it.

MR. HUDNUT. Oh, Hornblende is really afraid of life.
He tries to get out of himself but he's hopelessly introverted.
That's the real reason he's taken to living in Honduras. The
grandeur of the tropical coasts that he goes on about so
much has nothing whatever to do with it: what he's looking
for is a never-never land, where he can completely get away
from reality. His wife keeps house for him and does everything for him, and he lives in a continual daydream.

THE LADY. She's pretty awful, isn't she?

MR. HUDNUT. Oh, I like Edith: Edith's a good sort. Of
course, she's not terribly stimulating, but then, for the kind
of thing Bert wants, I suppose she's absolutely perfect. Bert
has a physical deformity, you know—one of his legs is shorter
than the other—and it has affected his whole point of view.
He's morbidly sensitive about it—he always sits with his
legs crossed, so that it won't be noticed. And when he's
photographed, he always makes a point of having the foot
of the longer leg on a step or a stump or something—or he's
standing on the side of a mountain. That's the reason he's
gone in for mountain-climbing. If Bert can be photographed
on the side of a mountain, with an alpenstock and a pretty
woman, he's perfectly happy—just like a child!

THE LADY. His wife doesn't make it particularly easy for him to see other women, I understand.

MR. HUDNUT. Yes: but her jealousy of poor old Bert is entirely unnecessary. He couldn't—or wouldn't—do anything even if she gave him a chance.

MR. BIRD (*continuing his story*). Well, Vide went over to the *Revue Libre,* which his brother-in-law Champfleury was founding, and the *Revue* began to boom Hornblende as the foremost American novelist, because Mme. Champfleury had translated his first novel. He has even been taken up by that unutterable sheet *Hurrah-Moche,* which is published by Lavarnier, who also publishes the *Revue Libre.* The young pro-American French aesthetes hailed Hornblende as one of the prophets of the literature of big machinery. That was before he had gone to Central America— a good joke on them! I wrote them a letter in French, with a translation of the back-to-the-wilderness outburst that he published just before he left. But they never either printed or replied to it. Perhaps they cannot read correct French. The very title of their magazine is gibberish! They have taken the English word "hurrah," which they have picked up and think very smart, and have affixed to it a French slang adjective. Together the two words mean nothing. It is nonsense! It is neither good French nor good English! An insult to the intelligence!

MR. HOSKINS (*speaking for the first time*). It seems to me that, in all this discussion of Hornblende, we have really failed so far to face the aesthetic problem he raises. I must say I disapprove of this habit, which seems to be becoming so prevalent, of making personal gossip do duty for an intellectual approach to literature. Hornblende's real weakness, it seems to me, becomes plain when we subject him to an aesthetic analysis. I begin by dividing works of literature into three clearly distinguishable classes, whose nature I can indicate best by an analogy from mathematics. I identify these three classes, also, with the three states of higher consciousness defined by Gundeljeff in his Eurasian yogi system. The first of these classes includes literary artists who represent some simple aesthetic entity multiplied by itself to a higher power—they correspond to the cubes, the squares and the other powers of algebra. Such writers are Victor Hugo, Horace, Metastasio, Milton and Trollope. This is Gundeljeff's ectogenetic state of consciousness: the words of art are given off by the artist from *the outside*. The third class is that which includes almost all the greatest figures in literature: it has its mathematical equivalent in the irrational numbers we call surds—that is, numbers that are not susceptible of having rational roots extracted—and its philosophical equivalent is the engenetic state of Gundeljeff: the work of art is gestated *within* the artist and never wholly emerges. Into this class fall Mallarmé, John Donne, Herman Melville, the author of the *Kalevala,* Oscar Pilseck and the best parts of Pindar. It was because we wished to insist upon this fundamental aspect of literature that Pilseck and myself have called our magazine $\sqrt{2}$, and, by resorting to a different technique of analysis from any that has yet been applied, we have been able to extract, to an approximation equivalent to ten places of decimals, the root of the aesthetic blend of elements—susceptible, of course, of a qualitative as well as a quantitative analysis—that, raised to the x power, have resulted in the work of art. Performing the inverse operation, we shall also be able to approximate the production of works of art of the irrational engenetic kind, and our essay in the first issue in reality provides prolegomena to the method of a new body of literature, in which what has hitherto been produced by the freaks and the flukes of individual genius will be forged by the application of a rigorous intellectual discipline. There is, however, a second intermediate class, to which Bertram Hornblende belongs—

The conversation is suddenly terminated by the downfall of Western civilization.

—Edmund Wilson

Chicago Letter

April, 1949

"Voyage infortuné! Rivage malheureux,
Falloit-il approcher de tes bords dangereux?"
—Racine

 Agony, a sense of plight; a sense of agony, plight—
such, one soon preceives, are the attributes of the Chicago
of our time. But I shall have more to say about them
later in this letter.

I traveled by the Erie, as one must, I think, do, now and
then. The trip is longer, to be sure, on its ancient twisting
right-of-way than on other roads. But there one escapes
the *"lumpenaristokratie"* (in Roscoe Chutney's phrase) of
the Century or the Broadway, and it is only from the Erie,
of course, that one may catch those extraordinary night
glimpses of Youngstown and Akron.

I had not planned to do much reading on the train, but
recalling how trying the journey could be (in certain weathers)
between Hankins and Horseheads, I had as a precaution
bought the latest *Peristalsis* at a kiosk in the Jersey City
station. It was thus, at lunch (in the diner) that I happened
upon Hjalmar Ekdal's essay, "Kafka's Ulcer"—a subject I
had outlined to Hjalmar at Ocean Grove in the late summer
of 1945. Had he quite *realized* it, though, in Cézanne's sense?
I could not, at the moment, be entirely certain.

Some hours later, settled in my berth (there is something
to be said for the old standard sleeper, after all), and glanc-

ing through the rest of the magazine (which [as it happened]
I had no clear intention of reading then), I discovered
Mildred's Belgrade Letter, Sam's Naples Letter, Boris's
Pskov Letter, Fred's Capetown Letter, Deirdre's Quito
Letter, Jaroslav's Paris Letter, and Harry's Prague Letter.
These were precisely the people I had looked forward most
to seeing in Chicago, and it was small comfort to be told
(on my arrival) of the fate already suffered by several of
them—Boris and Harry shot by Stalinists (on a trumped-up
charge of cosmopolitan rootlessness), Mildred hanged by
Titoists in the woods north of Slunj, Sam abducted by the
resurgent Mafia, Deirdre raped, robbed, and butchered by
Clerical-Trotskyists. How explain these horrors? Those
who remained in Chicago shrugged their shoulders in anxious
silence at my question. What was in store for others, who
has just left or were about to leave—Erma and Roscoe
Chutney, already on their way to Shiraz; the Ekdals, who
were departing the day after my arrival?

"It doesn't much matter where I go," Hjalmar told me.
"Hatred and envy are my shadows. I had thought of the
Yukon, God knows why, but Gina's already promised two
Aleppo Letters to *Peristalsis,* so I suppose we might as
well go there. Is it true that they still use the old water
torture in Aleppo? One might (at least) have that to look
forward to."

I could not tell him: I have not been in Aleppo since I
was eight or nine. All the same, I knew that Hjalmar was
suffering. Kafka's ulcer had, in some sense, become *his*
ulcer. Or, was the world his ulcer? Does our proper pleasure
in Kafka lie (after all) in this mutual *anagnorisis* of symptoms—in what I have ventured elsewhere[1] to describe as "an
act of critical nosology"?

I had not yet become aware of Hjalmar's torment when
Jens Kobold met me at Dearborn Station—where the grimy
Victorian interior has been entirely remodeled (I do not
allude, of course, to the trainshed, but to the waiting-rooms,

[1] "Criticism as Diagnosis." *Peristalsis,*
Winter-Summer, 1943.

ticket-counters, and so on) in what may best be called a sort of middle-upper-brow notion of "modern" *décor*. As for Jens, he seemed during the first few seconds much as ever—monolithic, *rébarbatif,* with that quality of tempered urgency which Roscoe Chutney has so profoundly pictured in *The Critical Stud-Book.* But as we drove through the rotting streets of the Loop and the Near North Side, I detected something new: he appeared discrete, shattered. His only reply to my questions was to spit from the taxi window and mumble an evasive phrase about riots in the Bosnian quarter. I could not imagine what he meant: there is always rioting in Chicago's Bosnian quarter, and Jens had always boasted his entire indifference to *la question Bosnienne.* For the moment I said no more, and contemplated the buildings and the hoardings. On one of these latter, an enormous photo-mural (of Truman Capote [I think] balanced perilously in ballet costume on a high wire) had already been savagely ripped by the lake wind. But worse was to come.

At Jens's studio pretty much all that was left of the *premier rang* of Chicago's *avant garde* was spiritlessly waiting for us: the Ekdals, appalled by the amount of packing still to be done and by the strawberry rash which Gina's ringworm shots had produced; Bernard Mosher, apprehensively drunk; George Barnwell, Máire Ní Laoghaire, Jeremy Irk (unshakeably gloomy, despite the putative success of his new play—of which more later).

The party was, of course, a desperate failure: I find it a torture to record my own corrosive memories of it. The lovely Máire no longer stretched on the floor with Jeremy to say wise, dreadful things about Dostoevsky; now she sat hunched and nearly silent on the Grand Rapids divan which is so familiar and amusing a shape in Jens's pictures of the '30's. As for the others—but why persist on this level of discourse? I sensed that much was missing—but what? Recently I had read somewhere that French intellectuals are gayer, less elegiac than their opposite numbers in America. I had not dreamed, however, that American intel-

lectuals are so little gay, so formidably elegiac. What was
the nexus?

In the course of that long, disenchanted first day in
Chicago I discovered that Jens had given up easel painting,
and that he now, in his phrase, "soils" pages torn at random
from the *Tribune,* at which he flings wildly-punctured cans
of ten-cent-store oil paint. The results are, of course, often
magnificent—Máire Ní Laoghaire has written superbly of
Jens's *jetage*—but all the same they hint (possibly) at something not far removed from uncertainty—an uncertainty even
more apparent in the work of those imitators of his who
have attempted the same sort of thing with the *Sun-Times*
or *Herald-American.* I cannot avoid being enormously
impressed by many of these new pictures of Jens's, yet I
find it not easy to conceive what is central to their strategy.
Jens himself, who once talked and wrote so copiously about
the nature of life and painting, labels them—almost hate-
fully—as "Tribunemalerei," and appears contemptuous of
the opinions of Máire, with whom (I am told) he is no
longer living.

It was Bernard Mosher who first found precise words for
what I had sensed of menace and despair in Chicago. "Call
it what you will," he said as we walked along Van Buren
Street after seeing the Ekdals off, "it is, in my phrase, 'a
sense of plight.'" At this point he left me abruptly (we had
reached the corner of Van Buren and Wells), and I turned
north in the shadow of the "L" for my first stroll in the
doomed city.

A casual visitor might not at first glance suspect the
tragic tension which torments Chicago's intellectuals and
artists. Trifles are taken for wonders: under the administration of Mayor Kennelly political corruption has ceased,
and what the philistine press calls "vice" has been driven
out (I have yet to meet a police reporter who truly appre-
hends the nature of original sin). Lake Michigan seems, on
the surface, unchanged. The same dingy pigeons swarm for
peanuts on the "L" platforms of the Loop, and the shabby
skyscrapers blot out the afternoon sun. The new streetcars

already look old (as everything new looks old in Chicago). Towards the end of the day they are filled, in monotonous ritual fashion, with anthropoid businessmen frowning heavily over the *Daily News,* and bored high-school girls carelessly swinging their eternal battered copies of *The Brothers Karamazov.* On Sundays humorless bourgeois families go picnicking in the fogs along the Drainage Canal, or watch passionless "play" of the White Sox or the Cubs (also gripped by plight—of [I suspect] a rather different order).

Little by little, as the leaden hours slog by in this joyless metropolis, one clutches at further tokens of the truth of Bernard Mosher's *aperçu.* I do not (of course) propose to burden this letter with statistics, but where are the great Chicago essays of the mid-1940-s?[2] Who, for example, writes about Melville now? Three years ago the mean annual production in Cook County of Melville books and articles was 274; today it is scarcely fifteen. Three years ago we were finding new hope in George Barnwell's "Melville's Whale and M. de Charlus," Hjalmar Ekdal's "Melville's Tumor," Bernard Mosher's "Barnwell, Ekdal, and the Melville World." Nowadays one encounters, at best—and it is simply not good enough—some Northwestern University pedant's cynical and barren, "Smile When You Call Me Ishmael." *Und weiter nichts.*

Other facts suggest the city's agony. A fortnight after my arrival I read in the *Cicero Quarterly* (which last week ceased publication) of the dissolution of the Goose Island Sartre Club, whose president, with ironic ambivalence, rather than commit suicide had taken a job as check-out boy in a supermarket. Early today, as I started to compose this letter, Jeremy Irk phoned to tell me that the Rogers Park *Cercle Rimbaud* is down to nine members, eight of whom do not speak to each other. Yet, with all this endemic apathy, one learns of eruptions of violence as well (I do not here allude to the Bosnian riots, of course). In the dim alleys

[2] One recalls, above all, perhaps, Irk and Chutney, "The Heresy of Fallacy" (*Peristalsis,* Winter-Summer, 1945); Chut- ney and Irk, "The Fallacy of Heresy" (*Peristalsis,* Winter-Summer, 1946).

of the South Side, I am told, "goon squads" from the Aristotle A.C. sally out after nightfall to sack hostile bookshops,
or worse. Such things are, to be sure, a kind of action, although I cannot say what hope one is to take from it.

It is along South State and North Clark streets that one
is most sharply conscious of the pervasive sense of plight.
Here, as in the past, one discovers the youth of the *avant
garde,* but now much altered—frustrated painters, *poètes
par trop manqués,* defeated composers, disappointed novelists,
exhausted sculptors, beaten playwrights, embittered critics,
bilious critics of critics, all of them shivering in the cold
spring rain, but too tired, indolent, indifferent to seek the
relative warmth of the bars. I do not propose to intrude
upon my readers that improbable figure of American myth,
the philosophical bartender, but I did chance upon one old
man—he had known Kierkegaard at Trondhjem, as it happened—who put the case for me about as clearly as anyone
else had done. I was watching him construct North Clark
street's favorite drink, a double *pousse-café,* and as he
worked at it with his precise artist's fingers, he nodded
through the door towards the crowds outside.

"These kids got the sense of plight so bad they ain't
even writing or talking about it, nor trying to reduce it
somehow to canvas or stone," he said. "You take as recent
as six, eight months ago they'd r'ar up and snap at each
other like they was Stanley Edgar Kazin. You know how
I mean—'Jake that dope he don't really unnerstand the
nature of Myth,' 'Mike, all the psychoanalysis he ever read,
if he ever read it, is Joseph Jastrow,' 'Moe combines ignorance
wit brashness to an amazing degree,' 'Joe's got about as
much innerest in the *text* of a poem—by which I mean *what*
a poem *is*—as a Van Buren street pigeon has in clean feath-
ers.' In there pitching. This joint used to sound like it was,
you might say, collective criticism by symposium going
on all the time. But what do they do now? Just set out there
in the rain on the *terrasse* and mope. I ain't even heard
Hemingway sneered at in rising two months. You looking
for the sense of plight, boy, you come to the right town!"

If plight has come close to silencing the artists and critics, it has (for all practical purposes) obliterated the philosophers and political theorists. A few, I gather, have entered general semantics, a few have killed themselves or each other. As for still others—

> *"Tout fuit; et sans s'armer d'un courage inutile,*
> *Dans le temple voisin chacun cherche un asile"*

in Racine's sense of the phrase. Only yesterday the Cafe Désespoir et du Terminus closed its doors. The Heidegger Bar and Grill has (I heard) taken to watering its *pousse-cafés*. Where is an answer to be found?

It is clearly not to be found in the Chicago theatre. In the commodity houses of the Loop one is faced (inevitably) with pure *Kitsch*—ill-made well-made plays, well-made ill-made plays, tepidly performed before drowsy lower-middle-brow audiences which wake into sudden anxious laughter at bathroom jokes, then sink back into the somnolence of the damned.

The best theatre in Chicago was available (I use "was" here in its sense of past tense of "to be") very distant from the Loop, in an abandoned warehouse on the Far Northwest Side, where one climbed four flights of condemned wooden stairs to a makeshift hall under a decaying roof. The second-hand seats in the orchestra, gnawed incessantly by rats, were scantily occupied by bewildered bourgeois couples and drunken slummers from the Gold Coast. The rickety balcony was packed with sullen students, who showed little interest in what was going on, little sign of the passion for theatre which may once have possessed them.

Máire Ní Laoghaire took me one night to see Jean-Jean Baroque act Jeremy Irk's *Les Voyeurs de Rogers Park,* in Irk's own extraordinary translation. This is (in some respects) a puzzling play, and until I have read the script, I shall not venture to pronounce a final judgment on it. "Mordant, plangent, repellent," (in Máire Ní Laoghaire's phrase) it is at once strikingly astringent, yet rather like warm marshmallows. There are eight acts (five of them,

of course, in verse) of which the first three, played in a
blackout, are almost hauntingly rhetorical. But more than
any other play I have seen in years (in London, Paris, New
York, Rome, Moscow, Stambouli, Narvik, that is), Irk's
drama comes to close grips with certain deeply imbedded
constituents of the American myth—particularly various
suburban *rites de passage* reminiscent—at first hearing, in
any event—of those which Rudge observed in Lower Borneo.
I am persuaded, however, that Irk's parallel between Salmon
P. Chase and the Corn God may be at once too tenuous
and too obvious.

But I shall not attempt to summarize the play here—
the fourth and seventh acts are to appear in the Winter-
Summer *Peristalsis*—because I wish to comment rather on
the amazing art of Baroque. An ugly little man, with a
whiskey baritone which engaged one like a wood rasp (I
have heard that he had been [at one time] a bouncer in the
Pump Room), he was able to transmute himself into an
entire world of characters, none of them conventional and
all of them complex. In the course of the action he was
by turns (one could almost swear simultaneously, and this
may, indeed, have been in large measure the *clef* of his
achievement) an existentialist high-school junior, a "bop"
xylophonist, a sentimental police sergeant, a sort of philosophy professor, a myopic anthropologist, Raskolnikov's
ghost, and the oldest sadist in Rogers Park. Baroque made
impressively little use of his body: "He seems," Máire Ní
Laoghaire told me, "somehow to do it all with his skin."
Did Baroque betray the sense of plight? There was no time
for me to ascertain an answer to this question.

It may, very possibly, have been a greater tragedy for the
Chicago stage, and for our decomposing culture in general,
than we yet realize, when (two days after my visit, as it
happened) the theatre suddenly caved in, and Baroque
(with his entire company), three bourgeois couples, a sodden
débutante and her elderly lover, innumerable rats, and the
balconyful of students were plunged four flights into a
flooded basement. All of them were crushed to death, or

drowned. I cannot (it seems to me) escape the conviction that this incident was a further token of the city's fate—perhaps (though, of course, by no means certainly) more momentous than most.

Jeremy Irk, staggered as he was by this occurrence, has not yet been able to complete his poem about it. But I was fortunate enough to inspect several fragments of the work in progress before they (together with Bernard Mosher's discussion of them) were shipped off to Buffalo, and I am privileged to announce that Irk's work is quite *indicible*. I had, of course, hoped to persuade Jeremy to allow their publication with this letter, but he refused with the tired, broken smile which he had learned so well from Jens Kobold's portrait of him.

"It's too late," he said, although I had pointed out to him that publication of his fragments might be one means of leading the city out of its plight.

"Too late . . . too late," he continued. (These words cling to one like lint in the Chicago of the mid-twentieth century.) "It is too late for too many things. Too late for Máire's film on Bernard Mosher. Too late for Gina's ballet, though the slippers have already been ordered. Too late for Erma Chutney's novel about our common predicament. It is too late for Roscoe Chutney's study of Hjalmar as critic, and for Hjalmar's monograph on Jens's lithographs. It is too late for George Barnwell to take issue with Roscoe. It is too late for Jens's note, with sketches, on Gina's choreography. It is, of course, much too late for Bernard's book on Máire. Like an arthritic juggler, one feels no longer able to keep the balls in the air. It is just too late."

I shall, perhaps, let these words of Jeremy's stand in this letter as a kind of epiphany, in the various senses of the word.

*   *   *

"On dit qu'un prompt départ vous éloigne de nous,
Seigneur."

—Racine

Tonight I propose to quit this crumbling city. I have just observed in the *Official Railway Guide* that the International Limited on the Grand Trunk leaves for Halifax at 8 p.m. But my copy of the *Guide* is dated November, 1944, and belongs, thus, one suspects, to another world The time may be wrong. Perhaps this train has been canceled. Perhaps the timetable of the Grand Trunk has achieved (at last) a fresh and more telling synthesis. Yet, if not this train, then another.

I shall not tell Máire, who has expressed a desire (which it would not [all things considered] be improper to call insistent) to go with me when I go. It might be rather amusing to show her the bleak old city on its crags, to introduce her to the *avant garde* of Nova Scotia. But I cannot risk carrying any part of Chicago with me: I take it that my Halifax Letter must concern itself with Halifax *as* Halifax.

Perhaps there too I shall encounter a sense of plight. Perhaps it is not limited to Chicago or to Halifax. One wonders about these things as one packs, looking out of one's window at the slaty April sky of Chicago, at the lethargic gulls sagging listlessly towards the bruise-colored lake. One wonders. But one cannot, of course, be quite sure.

—*W. B. Scott*

Coda

»»»»»

Dover Beach

by Matthew Arnold

The sea is calm tonight.
The tide is full, the moon lies fair
Upon the straits;—on the French coast the light
Gleams and is gone; the cliffs of England stand,
Glimmering and vast, out in the tranquil bay.
Come to the window, sweet is the night-air!
Only, from the long line of spray
Where the sea meets the moon-blanched land,
Listen! you hear the grating roar
Of pebbles which the waves draw back, and fling,
At their return, up the high strand,
Begin, and cease, and then again begin,
With tremulous cadence slow, and bring
The eternal note of sadness in.

Sophocles long ago
Heard it on the Aegean, and it brought
Into his mind the turbid ebb and flow
Of human misery; we
Find also in the sound a thought,
Hearing it by this distant northern sea.

The Sea of Faith
Was once, too, at the full, and round earth's shore
Lay like the folds of a bright girdle furl'd.
But now I only hear

Its melancholy, long, withdrawing roar,
Retreating, to the breath
Of the night-wind, down the vast edges drear
And naked shingles of the world.

Ah, love, let us be true
To one another! for the world, which seems
To lie before us like a land of dreams,
So various, so beautiful, so new,
Hath really neither joy, nor love, nor light,
Nor certitude, nor peace, nor help for pain;
And we are here as on a darkling plain
Swept with confused alarms of struggle and flight,
Where ignorant armies clash by night.

Dover Beach Revisited
A New Fable for Critics

━━

∽ Early in the year 1939 a certain Professor of Educational Psychology, occupying a well-paid chair at a large endowed university, conceived a plot. From his desk in the imposing Hall of the Social Sciences where the Research Institute in Education was housed he had long burned with resentment against teachers of literature, especially against English departments. It seemed to him that the professors of English stood square across the path of his major professional ambition. His great desire in life was to introduce into the study, the teaching, the critical evaluation of literature some of the systematic method, some of the "objective procedure" as he liked to call it, some of the certainty of result which he believed to be characteristic of the physical sciences. "You make such a fetish of science," a colleague once said to him, "why aren't you a chemist?"— a question that annoyed him deeply.

If such a poem as Milton's "Lycidas" has a value—and most English teachers, even to-day, would start with that as a cardinal fact—then that value must be measurable and expressible in terms that do not shift and change from moment to moment and person to person with every subjective whim. They would agree, these teachers of literature, these professors of English, that the value of the poem is in some sense objective; they would never agree to undertake any objective procedure to determine what that value is. They would not clearly define what they meant by achievement in the study of literature, and they bridled and snorted when anyone else attempted to define it. He remembered what had happened when he had once been incautious enough to suggest to a professor of English in his own college that it might be possible to establish norms for the appreciation of Milton. The fellow had simply exploded into a peal of histrionic laughter and then had tried to wither him with an equally histrionic look of incredulity and disgust.

He would like to see what would happen if the teachers of English were forced or lured, by some scheme or other, into a public exposure of their position. It would put them in the light of intellectual charlatanism, nothing less . . . and suddenly Professor Chartly (for so he was nicknamed) began to see his way.

It was a simple plan that popped into his head, simple yet bold and practical. It was a challenge that could not be refused. A strategically placed friend in one of the large educational foundations could be counted on: there would be money for clerical expenses, for travel if need be. He took his pipe from his pocket, filled it, and began to puff exultantly. To-morrow he must broach the scheme to one or two colleagues; to-night, over cheese and beer, would not be too soon. He reached for the telephone.

The plan that he unfolded to his associates that evening aroused considerable skepticism at first, but gradually they succumbed to his enthusiasm. A number of well-known professors of literature at representative colleges up and down the land would be asked to write a critical evaluation of a poem prominent enough to form part of the standard reading in all large English courses. They would be asked to state the criteria on which they based their judgment. When all the answers had been received the whole dossier would be sent to a moderator, a trusted elder statesman of education, known everywhere for his dignity, liberality of intelligence, and long experience. He would be asked to make a preliminary examination of all the documents and

to determine from the point of view of a teacher of literature whether they provided any basis for a common understanding. The moderator would then forward all the documents to Professor Chartly, who would make what in his
own mind he was frank to call a more scientific analysis.
Then the jaws of the trap would be ready to spring.

Once the conspirators had agreed on their plot their
first difficulty came in the choice of a poem. Suffice it to
say that someone eventually hit on Arnold's "Dover Beach,"
and the suggestion withstood all attack. "Dover Beach" was
universally known, almost universally praised; it was remote
enough so that contemporary jealousies and cults were not
seriously involved, yet near enough not to call for any special
expertness, historical or linguistic, as a prerequisite for judgment; it was generally given credit for skill as a work of
art, yet it contained also, in its author's own phrase, a
"criticism of life."

Rapidly in the days following the first meeting the representative teachers were chosen and invited to participate
in the plan. Professional courtesy seemed to require the
inclusion of an Arnold expert. But the one selected excused
himself from producing a value judgment of "Dover Beach"
on the ground that he was busy investigating a fresh clue
to the identity of "Marguerite." He had evidence that the
woman in question, after the episode hinted at in the famous
poems, had married her deceased sister's husband, thus
perhaps affecting Arnold's views on a social question about
which he had said a good deal in his prose writings. The
expert pointed out that he had been given a half-year's
leave of absence and a research grant to pursue the shadow
of Marguerite through Europe, wherever it might lead him.
If only war did not break out he hoped to complete his
research and solve one of the vexing problems that had
always confronted Arnold's biographers. His energies would
be too much engaged in this special investigation to deal
justly with the more general questions raised by Professor
Chartly's invitation. But he asked to be kept informed, since
the results of the experiment could not fail to be of interest
to him.

After a few hitches and delays from other quarters, the scheme was ripe. The requests were mailed out, and the Professor of Educational Psychology sat back in grim confidence to await the outcome.

II

It chanced that the first of the representative teachers who received and answered Professor Chartly's letter was thought of on his own campus as giving off a distinct though not unpleasant odor of the ivory tower. He would have resented the imputation himself. At forty-five Bradley Dewing was handsome in a somewhat speciously virile style, graying at the temples, but still well-knit and active. He prided himself on being able to beat most of his students at tennis; once a year he would play the third or fourth man on the varsity and go down to creditable defeat with some elegiac phrases on the ravages of time. He thought of himself as a man of the world; it was well for his contentment, which was seldom visibly ruffled, that he never heard the class mimic reproducing at a fraternity house or beer parlor his manner of saying: "After all, gentlemen, it is pure poetry that lasts. We must never forget the staying power of pure art." The class mimic never represents the whole of class opinion but he can usually make everyone within earshot laugh.

Professor Dewing could remember clearly what his own teachers had said about "Dover Beach" in the days when he was a freshman in college himself, phrases rounded with distant professorial unction: faith and doubt in the Victorian era; disturbing influence of Darwin on religious belief; Browning the optimist; Tennyson coming up with firm faith after a long struggle in the waters of doubt; Matthew Arnold, prophet of skepticism. How would "Dover Beach" stack up now as a poem? Pull Arnold down from the shelf and find out.

Ah, yes, how the familiar phrases came back. The sea is

calm, the tide is full, the cliffs of England stand . . . And
then the lines he particularly liked:

> Come to the window, sweet is the night-air!
> Only, from the long line of spray
> Where the sea meets the moon-blanch'd land,
> Listen! you hear the grating roar
> Of pebbles which the waves draw back, and fling,
> At their return, up the high strand,
> Begin, and cease, and then again begin,
> With tremulous cadence slow . . .

Good poetry, that! No one could mistake it. Onomatopoeia
was a relatively cheap effect most of the time. Poe, for
instance: "And the silken sad uncertain rustling of each
purple curtain." Anyone could put a string of s's together
and make them rustle. But these lines in "Dover Beach"
were different. The onomatopoeia was involved in the whole
scene, and it in turn involved the whole rhythmical movement of the verse, not the mere noise made by the conso-
nants or vowels as such. The pauses—only, listen, draw
back, fling, begin, cease—how they infused a subdued melancholy into the moonlit panorama at the same time that
they gave it the utmost physical reality by suggesting the
endless iteration of the waves! And then the phrase "With
tremulous cadence slow" coming as yet one more touch,
one "fine excess," when it seemed that every phrase and
pause the scene could bear had already been lavished on
it: that was Miltonic, Virgilian.

But the rest of the poem?

> The Sea of Faith
> Was once, too, at the full, and round earth's shore
> Lay like the folds of a bright girdle furl'd . . .

Of course Arnold had evoked the whole scene only to bring
before us this metaphor of faith in its ebb-tide. But that did
not save the figure from triteness and from an even more
fatal vagueness. Everything in second-rate poetry is compared to the sea: love is as deep, grief as salty, passion as
turbulent. The sea may look like a bright girdle sometimes,

though Professor Dewing did not think it particularly impressive to say so. And in what sense is *faith* a bright girdle? Is it the function of faith to embrace, to bind, to hold up a petticoat, or what? And what is the faith that Arnold has in mind? The poet evokes no precise concept of it. He throws us the simple, undifferentiated word, unites its loose emotional connotations with those of the sea, and leaves the whole matter there. And the concluding figure of "Dover Beach":

> we are here as on a darkling plain
> Swept with confused alarms of struggle and flight,
> Where ignorant armies clash by night.

Splendid in itself, this memorable image. But the sea had been forgotten now; the darkling plain had displaced the figure from which the whole poem tacitly promised to evolve. It would not have been so if John Donne had been the craftsman. A single bold yet accurate analogy, with constantly developing implications, would have served him for the whole poem.

Thus mused Professor Dewing, the lines of his verdict taking shape in his head. A critic of poetry of course was not at liberty to pass judgment on a poet's thought; he could only judge whether, in treating of the thought or sensibility he had received from his age, the poet had produced a satisfactory work of art. Arnold, Professor Dewing felt, had not been able to escape from the didactic tone or from a certain commonness and vagueness of expression. With deep personal misgivings about his position in a world both socially and spiritually barbarous, he had sought an image for his emotion, and had found it in the sea—a natural phenomenon still obscured by the drapings of conventional beauty and used by all manner of poets to express all manner of feelings. "Dover Beach" would always remain notable, Professor Dewing decided, as an expression of Victorian sensibility. It contained lines of ever memorable poetic skill. But it could not, he felt, be accepted as a uniformly satisfactory example of poetic art.

III

It was occasionally a source of wonder to those about him just why Professor Oliver Twitchell spent so much time and eloquence urging that man's lower nature must be repressed, his animal instincts kept in bounds by the exertion of the higher will. To the casual observer, Professor Twitchell himself did not seem to possess much animal nature. It seemed incredible that a desperate struggle with powerful bestial passions might be going on at any moment within his own slight frame, behind his delicate white face in which the most prominent feature was the octagonal glasses that focused his eyes on the outside world. Professor Twitchell was a good deal given to discipleship but not much to friendship. He had himself been a disciple of the great Irving Babbitt, and he attracted a small number of disciples among his own more earnest students. But no one knew him well. Only one of his colleagues, who took a somewhat sardonic interest in the mysteries of human nature, possessed a possible clue to the origin of his efforts to repress man's lower nature and vindicate his higher. This colleague had wormed his way sufficiently into Oliver Twitchell's confidence to learn about his family, which he did not often mention. Professor Twitchell, it turned out, had come of decidedly unacademic stock. One of his brothers was the chief salesman for a company that made domestic fire-alarm appliances. At a moment's notice he would whip out a sample from his bag or pocket, plug it into the nearest electric outlet, and while the bystanders waited in terrified suspense, would explain that in the dead of night, if the house caught fire, the thing would go off with a whoop loud enough to warn the soundest sleeper. Lined up with his whole string of brothers and sisters, all older than he, all abounding in spirits, Professor Twitchell looked like the runt of the litter. His colleague decided that he must have had a very hard childhood, and that it was not his own animal nature that he needed so constantly to repress, but his family's.

Whatever the reasons, Professor Twitchell felt no reality in the teaching of literature except as he could extract from it definitions and illustrations of man's moral struggle in the world. For him recent history had been a history of intellectual confusion and degradation, and hence of social confusion and degradation. Western thought had fallen into a heresy. It had failed to maintain the fundamental grounds of a true humanism. It had blurred the distinction between man, God, and nature. Under the influence of the sciences, it had set up a monism in which the moral as well as the physical constitution of man was included within nature and the laws of nature. It had, therefore, exalted man as naturally good, and exalted the free expression of all his impulses. What were the results of this heresy? An age, complained Professor Twitchell bitterly, in which young women talked about sexual perversions at the dinner table; an age in which everyone agreed that society was in dissolution and insisted on the privilege of being dissolute; an age without any common standards of value in morals or art; an age, in short, without discipline, without self-restraint in private life or public.

Oliver Twitchell when he received Professor Chartly's envelope sat down with a strong favorable predisposition toward his task. He accepted whole-heartedly Arnold's attitude toward literature: the demand that poetry should be serious, that it should present us with a criticism of life, that it should be measured by standards not merely personal, but in some sense *real*.

"Dover Beach" had become Arnold's best-known poem, admired as his masterpiece. It would surely contain, therefore, a distillation of his attitude. Professor Twitchell pulled down his copy of Arnold and began to read; and as he read he felt himself overtaken by surprised misgiving. The poem began well enough. The allusion to Sophocles, who had heard the sound of the retreating tide by the Aegean centuries ago, admirably prepared the groundwork of high seriousness for a poem which would culminate in a real

criticism of human experience. But did the poem so culminate? It was true that the world

> Hath really neither joy, nor love, nor light,
> Nor certitude, nor peace, nor help for pain

if one meant the world as the worldling knows it, the man
who conducts his life by unreflective natural impulse. Such
a man will soon enough encounter the disappointments of
ambition, the instability of all bonds and ties founded on
nothing firmer than passion or self-interest. But this incertitude of the world, to a true disciple of culture, should become a means of self-discipline. It should lead him to ask
how life may be purified and ennobled, how we may by
wisdom and self-restraint oppose to the accidents of the world
a true human culture based on the exertion of a higher will.
No call to such a positive moral will, Professor Twitchell
reluctantly discovered, can be heard in "Dover Beach." Man
is an ignorant soldier struggling confusedly in a blind battle. Was this the culminating truth that Arnold the poet
had given men in his masterpiece? Professor Twitchell
sadly revised his value-judgment of the poem. He could
not feel that in his most widely admired performance Arnold
had seen life steadily or seen it whole; rather he had seen
it only on its worldly side, and seen it under an aspect of
terror. "Dover Beach" would always be justly respected for
its poetic art, but the famous lines on Sophocles better
exemplified the poet as a critic of life.

IV

As a novelist still referred to in his late thirties as "young"
and "promising," Rudolph Mole found himself in a curious
relation toward his academic colleagues. He wrote for the
public, not for the learned journals; hence he was spared
the necessity of becoming a pedant. At the same time the
more lucrative fruits of pedantry were denied to him by
his quiet exclusion from the guild. Younger men sweating
for promotion, living in shabby genteel poverty on yearly

appointments, their childless wives mimicking their academic shop-talk in bluestocking phrases, would look up from the stacks of five-by-three cards on which they were constantly accumulating notes and references, and would say to him, "You don't realize how lucky you are, teaching composition. You aren't expected to know anything." Sometimes an older colleague, who had passed through several stages of the mysteries of preferment, would belittle professional scholarship to him with an elaborate show of graciousness and envy. "We are all just pedants," he would say. "You teach the students what they really want and need." Rudolph noticed that the self-confessed pedant went busily on publishing monographs and being promoted, while he himself remained, year by year, the English Department's most eminent poor relation.

He was not embittered. His dealings with students were pleasant and interesting. There was a sense of reality and purpose in trying to elicit from them a better expression of their thoughts, trying to increase their understanding of the literary crafts. He could attack their minds on any front he chose, and he could follow his intellectual hobbies as freely as he liked, without being confined to the artificial boundaries of a professional field of learning.

Freud, for example. When Professor Chartly and his accomplices decided that a teacher of creative writing should be included in their scheme and chose Rudolph Mole for the post, they happened to catch him at the height of his enthusiasm for Freud. Not that he expected to psychoanalyze authors through their works; that, he avowed, was not his purpose. You can't deduce the specific secrets of a man's life, he would cheerfully admit, by trying to fit his works into the text-book patterns of complexes and psychoses. The critic, in any case, is interested only in the man to the extent that he is involved in his work. But everyone agrees, Rudolph maintained, that the man is involved in his work. Some part of the psychic constitution of the author finds expression in every line that he writes. We can't understand the work unless we can understand the psychic traits that have gained expression in it. We may never be able to trace back these traits to their ultimate sources and causes, probably buried deep in the author's childhood. But we need to gain as much light on them as we can, since they appear in the work we are trying to apprehend, and determine its character. This is what criticism has always sought to do. Freud simply brings new light to the old task.

Rudolph was fortunate enough at the outset to pick up at the college bookstore a copy of Mr. Lionel Trilling's recent study of Matthew Arnold. In this volume he found much of his work already done for him. A footnote to Mr. Trilling's text, citing evidence from Professors Tinker and Lowry, made it clear that "Dover Beach" may well have been written in 1850, some seventeen years before it was first published. This, for Rudolph's purposes, was a priceless discovery. It meant that all the traditional talk about the poem was largely null and void. The poem was not a repercussion of the bombshell that Darwin dropped on the religious sensibilities of the Victorians. It was far more deeply personal and individual than that. Perhaps when Arnold published it his own sense of what it expressed or how it would be understood had changed. But clearly the poem came into being as an expression of what Arnold felt to be the particular kind of affection and passion he needed from a woman. It was a love poem, and took its place with utmost naturalness, once the clue had been given, in the group of similar and related poems addressed to "Marguerite." Mr. Trilling summed up in a fine sentence one strain in these poems, and the principal strain in "Dover Beach," when he wrote that for Arnold "fidelity is a word relevant only to those lovers who see the world as a place of sorrow and in their common suffering require the comfort of constancy."

> Ah, love, let us be true
> To one another! for the world . . .
> Hath really neither joy, nor love, nor light . . .

The point was unmistakable. And from the whole group
of poems to which "Dover Beach" belonged, a sketch of
Arnold as an erotic personality could be derived. The question whether a "real Marguerite" existed was an idle one, for
the traits that found expression in the poems were at least
"real" enough to produce the poems and to determine their
character.

And what an odd spectacle it made, the self-expressed
character of Arnold as a lover! The ordinary degree of aggres-
siveness, the normal joy of conquest and possession, seemed
to be wholly absent from him. The love he asked for was
essentially a protective love, sisterly or motherly; in its
unavoidable ingredient of passion he felt a constant danger,
which repelled and unsettled him. He addressed Marguerite
as "My sister!" He avowed and deplored his own womanish
fits of instability:

> I too have wish'd, no woman more,
> This starting, feverish heart, away.

He emphasized his nervous anguish and contrary impulses.
He was a "teas'd o'erlabour'd heart," "an aimless unallay'd
Desire." He could not break through his fundamental isola-
tion and submerge himself in another human soul, and he
believed that all men shared this plight:

> Yes: in the sea of life enisl'd,
> With echoing straits between us thrown,
> Dotting the shoreless watery wild,
> We mortal millions live *alone*.

He never "without remorse" allowed himself

> To haunt the place where passions reign,

yet it was clear that whether he had ever succeeded in
giving himself up wholeheartedly to a passion, he had wanted
to. There could hardly be a more telltale phrase than "Once-
long'd-for storms of love."

In short much more illumination fell on "Dover Beach"
from certain other verses of Arnold's than from Darwin
and all his commentators:

> Truth—what is truth? Two bleeding hearts
> Wounded by men, by Fortune tried,
> Outwearied with their lonely parts,
> Vow to beat henceforth side by side.
>
> The world to them was stern and drear;
> Their lot was but to weep and moan.
> Ah, let them keep their faith sincere,
> For neither could subsist alone!

Here was the nub. "Dover Beach" grew directly from and repeated the same emotion, but no doubt generalized and enlarged this emotion, sweeping into one intense and far-reaching conviction of insecurity not only Arnold's personal fortunes in love, but the social and religious faith of the world he lived in. That much could be said for the traditional interpretation.

Of course, as Mr. Trilling did not fail to mention, anguished love affairs, harassed by mysterious inner incompatibilities, formed a well-established literary convention. But the fundamental sense of insecurity in "Dover Beach" was too genuine, too often repeated in other works, to be written off altogether to that account. The same sense of insecurity, the same need for some rock of protection, cried out again and again, not merely in Arnold's love poems but in his elegies, reflective pieces, and fragments of epic as well. Whenever Arnold produced a genuine and striking burst of poetry, with the stamp of true self-expression on it, he seemed always to be in the dumps. Everywhere dejection, confusion, weakness, contention of soul. No adequate cause could be found in the events of Arnold's life for such an acute sense of incertitude; it must have been of psychic origin. Only in one line of effort this fundamental insecurity did not hamper, sadden, or depress him, and that was in the free play of his intelligence as a critic of letters and society. Even there, if it did not hamper his efforts, it directed them. Arnold valiantly tried to erect a barrier of culture against the chaos and squalor of society, against the contentiousness of men. What was this barrier but an elaborate protective device?

The origin of the psychic pattern that expressed itself in Arnold's poems could probably never be discovered. No doubt the influence that Arnold's father exercised over his emotions and his thinking, even though Arnold rebelled to the extent at least of casting off his father's religious beliefs, was of great importance. But much more would have to be known to give a definite clue—more than ever could be known. Arnold was secure from any attempt to spy out the heart of his mystery. But if criticism could not discover the cause, it could assess the result, and could do so (thought Rudolph Mole) with greater understanding by an attempt, with up-to-date psychological aid, to delve a little deeper into the essential traits that manifested themselves in that result.

V

In 1917 Reuben Hale, a young instructor in a Western college, had lost his job and done time in the penitentiary for speaking against conscription and for organizing pacifist demonstrations. In the twenties he had lost two more academic posts for his sympathies with Soviet Russia and his inability to forget his Marxist principles while teaching literature. His contentious, eager, lovable, exasperating temperament tried the patience of one college administration after another. As he advanced into middle age, and his growing family suffered repeated upheavals, his friends began to fear that his robust quarrels with established order would leave him a penniless outcast at fifty. Then he was invited to take a flattering post at a girls' college known for its liberality of views. The connection proved surprisingly durable; in fact it became Professor Hale's turn to be apprehensive. He began to be morally alarmed at his own security, to fear that the bourgeois system which he had attacked so valiantly had somehow outwitted him and betrayed him into allegiance. When the C.I.O. made its initial drive and seemed to be carrying everything before it, he did his best to unseat himself again by rushing joyfully to the nearest picket lines and getting himself photographed by an alert press. Even this expedient failed, and he reconciled himself, not without wonder, to apparent academic permanence.

On winter afternoons his voice could be heard booming out through the closed door of his study to girls who came to consult him on all manner of subjects, from the merits of Plekhanov as a Marxist critic to their own most personal dilemmas. They called him Ben; he called them Smith, Jones, and Robinson. He never relaxed his cheerful bombardment of the milieu into which they were born, and of the larger social structure which made bourgeois wealth, bourgeois art, morals, and religion possible. But when a sophomore found herself pregnant it was to Professor Hale that she came for advice. Should she have an abortion or go through with it and heroically bear the social stigma? And it was Professor Hale who kept the affair from the Dean's office and the newspapers, sought out the boy, persuaded the young couple that they were desperately in love with each other, and that pending the revolution a respectable marriage would be the most prudent course, not to say the happiest.

James Joyce remarks of one of his characters that she dealt with moral problems as a cleaver deals with meat. Professor Hale's critical methods were comparably simple and direct. Literature, like the other arts, is in form and substance a product of society, and reflects the structure of society. The structure of society is a class structure: it is conditioned by the mode of production of goods, and by the legal conventions of ownership and control by which the ruling class keeps itself in power and endows itself with the necessary freedom to exploit men and materials for profit. A healthy literature, in a society so constituted, can exist only if writers perceive the essential economic problem and ally themselves firmly with the working class.

Anyone could see the trouble with Arnold. His intelligence revealed to him the chaos that disrupted the society about him; the selfishness and brutality of the ruling class; the

ugliness of the world which the industrial revolution had
created, and which imperialism and "liberalism" were extend-
ing. Arnold was at his best in his critical satire of this
world and of the ignorance of those who governed it. But
his intelligence far outran his will, and his defect of will
finally blinded his intelligence. He was too much a child
of his class to disown it and fight his way to a workable
remedy for social injustice. He caught a true vision of himself
and of his times as standing between "two worlds, one dead,
one powerless to be born." But he had not courage or stomach enough to lend his own powers to the birth struggle. Had
he thrown in his sympathies unreservedly with the working
class, and labored for the inescapable revolution, "Dover
Beach" would not have ended in pessimism and confusion. It
would have ended in a cheerful, strenuous, and hopeful call
to action. But Arnold could not divorce himself from the
world of polite letters, of education, of culture, into which
he had been born. He did his best to purify them, to make
them into an instrument for the reform of society. But
instinctively he knew that "culture" as he understood the
term was not a social force in the world around him. Instinctively he knew that what he loved was doomed to defeat.
And so "Dover Beach" ended in a futile plea for protection
against the hideousness of the darkling plain and the confused alarms of struggle and flight.

Professor Chartly's envelope brought Reuben Hale his
best opportunity since the first C.I.O. picket lines to vindicate his critical and social principles. He plunged into
his answer with complete zest.

VI

When Peter Lee Prampton agreed to act as moderator
in Professor Chartly's experiment he congratulated himself
that this would be his last great academic chore. He had
enjoyed his career of scholarship and teaching, no man ever
more keenly. But now it was drawing to an end. He was
loaded with honors from two continents. The universities

of Germany, France, and Britain had first laid their forma-
tive hands on his learning and cultivation, then given their
most coveted recognition to its fruits. But the honor and
the glory seemed a little vague on the June morning when
the expressman brought into his library the sizable package
of papers which Professor Chartly had boxed and shipped
to him. He had kept all his life a certain simplicity of heart.
At seventy-four he could still tote a pack with an easy
endurance that humiliated men of forty. Now he found himself giving in more and more completely to a lust for trout.
Half a century of hastily snatched vacations in Cape Breton
or the Scottish Highlands had never allowed him really
to fill up that hollow craving to find a wild stream and
fish it which would sometimes rise in his throat even in the
midst of a lecture.

Well, there would be time left before he died. And meanwhile here was this business of "Dover Beach." Matthew
Arnold during one of his American lecture tours had been
entertained by neighbors of the Pramptons. Peter Lee
Prampton's father had dined with the great man, and had
repeated his conversation and imitated his accent at the
family table. Peter himself, as a boy of nineteen or so, had
gone to hear Arnold lecture. That, he thought with a smile,
was probably a good deal more than could be said for any
of these poor hacks who had taken Professor Chartly's
bait.

At the thought of Arnold he could still hear the carriage
wheels grate on the pebbly road as he had driven, fifty
odd years ago, to the lecture in town, the prospective Mrs.
Prampton beside him. His fishing rod lay under the seat.
He chuckled out loud as he remembered how a pound-and-
a-half trout had jumped in the pool under the clattering
planks of the bridge, and how he had pulled up the horse,
jumped out, and tried a cast while Miss Osgood sat scolding
in the carriage and shivering in the autumn air. They had
been just a little late reaching the lecture, but the trout,
wrapped in damp leaves, lay safely beside the rod.

It was queer that "Dover Beach" had not come more

recently into his mind. Now that he turned his thoughts in that direction the poem was there in its entirely, waiting to be put on again like a coat that one has worn many times with pleasure and accidentally neglected for a while.

> The Sea of Faith
> Was once, too, at the full . . .

How those old Victorian battles had raged about the Prampton table when he was a boy! How the names of Arnold, Huxley, Darwin, Carlyle, Morris, Ruskin had been pelted back and forth by the excited disputants! *Literature and Dogma, God and the Bible, Culture and Anarchy.* The familiar titles brought an odd image into his mind: the tall figure of his father stretching up to turn on the gas lamps in the evening as the family sat down to dinner; the terrific pop of the pilot light as it exploded into a net of white flame, shaped like a little beehive; the buzz and whine of a jet turned up too high.

> Ah, love, let us be true
> To one another! for the world, which seems
> To lie before us like a land of dreams,
> So various, so beautiful, so new,
> Hath really neither joy, nor love, nor light,
> Nor certitude, nor peace, nor help for pain . . .

Peter Lee Prampton shivered in the warmth of his sunny library, shivered with that flash of perception into the past which sometimes enables a man to see how all that has happened in his life, for good or ill, turned on the narrowest edge of chance. He lived again in the world of dreams that his own youth had spread before him, a world truly vari-, ous, beautiful, and new; full of promise, adventure, and liberty of choice, based on the opportunities which his father's wealth provided, and holding out the prospect of a smooth advance into a distinguished career. Then, within six months, a lavish demonstration that the world has neither certitude, nor peace, nor help for pain: his mother's death by cancer, his father's financial overthrow and suicide, the ruin of his own smooth hopes and the prospect instead of a long, hampered, and obscure fight toward his perhaps impossible ambition. He lived again through the night hours when he had tramped out with himself the youthful question whether he could hold Miss Osgood to her promise in the face of such reversals. And he did not forget how she took his long-sleepless face between her hands, kissed him, and smiled away his anxiety with unsteady lips. Surely everyone discovers at some time or other that the world is not a place of certitude; surely everyone cries out to some other human being for the fidelity which alone can make it so. What more could be asked of a poet than to take so profound and universal an experience and turn it into lines that could still speak long after he and his age were dead?

The best of it was that no one could miss the human feeling, the cry from the heart, in "Dover Beach"; it spoke so clearly and eloquently, in a language everyone could understand, in a form classically pure and simple. Or did it? Who could tell what any job-lot of academicians might be trusted to see or fail to see? And this assortment in Chartly's package might be a queer kettle of fish! Peter Lee Prampton had lived through the *Yellow Book* days of Art for Art's sake; he had read the muckrakers, and watched the rise of the Marxists and the Freudians. Could "Dover Beach" be condemned as unsympathetic with labor? Could a neurosis or a complex be discovered in it? His heart sank at the sharp sudden conviction that indeed these and worse discoveries about the poem might be seriously advanced. Well, he had always tried to go on the principle that every school of criticism should be free to exercise any sincere claim on men's interest and attention which it could win for itself. When he actually applied himself to the contents of Professor Chartly's bale he would be as charitable as he could, as receptive to light from any quarter as he could bring himself to be.

But the task could wait. He felt the need of a period of adjustment before he could approach it with reasonable equanimity. And in the meanwhile he could indulge himself in some long-needed editorial work on his dry-fly book.

—Theodore Morrison

Contributors to This Issue

∾ Unfortunately the current issue of our magazine has had to be abandoned because of low visibility and an epidemic of printers' nausea, but we felt that our readers would still want to know a little something of the private lives of our contributors. At any rate, here we go:

ELWOOD M. CRINGE, who contributed the article *Is Europe?* is a graduate of Moffard College and, since graduation, has specialized in high tension rope. He is thirty-two years old, wears a collar, and his hobbies are golf, bobbing for apples, and junket.

HAL GARMISCH, author of *How It Feels to Be Underslung*, writes: "I am young, good-looking and would like to meet a girl about my own age who likes to run. I have no hobbies, but I am crazy about kitties."

MEDFORD LAZENBY probably knows more about people, as such, than anyone in the country, unless it is people themselves. He has been all over the world in a balloon-rigged ketch and has a fascinating story to tell. *China Through a Strainer,* in this issue, is not it.

ELIZABETH FEDELLER, after graduation from Ruby College for Near-Sighted Girls, had a good time for herself among the deserted towns of Montana and writes of her experiences in a style which has been compared unfavorably with that of Ernest Hemingway. She is rather unattractive looking.

On our request for information, GIRLIE TENNAFLY wrote us that he is unable to furnish any, owing to a short memory.

He contributed the article on *Flanges: Open and Shut,* which is not appearing in this issue.

We will let ESTHER RUBRIC tell about herself: "Strange as it may seem," writes Miss Rubric, "I am not a 'high-brow', although I write on what are known as 'high-brow' subjects. I am really quite a good sport, and love to play tennis (or 'play at' tennis, as I call it), and am always ready for a good romp. My mother and father were missionaries in Boston, and I was brought up in a strictly family way. We children used to be thought strange by all the other 'kids' in Boston because my brothers had beards and I fell down a lot. But, as far as I can see, we all grew up to be respectable citizens, in a pig's eye. When your magazine accepted my article on *How to Decorate a Mergenthaler Linotype Machine,* I was in the 'seventh heaven.' I copied it, word for word, from Kipling."

DARG GAMM is too well known to our readers to call for an introduction. He is now at work on his next-but-one novel and is in hiding with the Class of 1915 of Zanzer College, who are preparing for their twentieth reunion in June.

We couldn't get IRVIN S. COBB or CLARENCE BUDINGTON KELLAND to answer our request for manuscripts.

—Robert Benchley

Our Contributors

(*This time for real*)

〜〉 Richard Armour, former dean at Scripps College, is the author of many volumes of humor and of light verse . . . The late Robert Benchley was a drama critic, film actor, and one of America's best-known humorists . . . Wayne Booth is Professor of English and Dean of the College at the University of Chicago . . . Jorge Luis Borges, poet, essayist and critic, is director of the Argentine National Library . . . Douglas Bush is Professor of English at Harvard University . . . Robert Conquest is a British poet, critic, and political writer . . . Herbert C. Coursen, Jr., teaches English at Bowdoin College . . . Frederick C. Crews is Professor of English at the University of California (Berkeley) . . . Charles V. Genthe teacher English at Chico State College . . . John Halverson teaches English at the University of California (Santa Cruz) . . . Bruce Harkness is Dean of Liberal Arts at Kent State University . . . Charles Kaplan is Professor of English at San Fernando Valley State College . . . Felicia Lamport lives in Cambridge, Massachusetts, and contributes satire and light verse to leading popular magazines . . . Theodore Morrison is Professor of English at Harvard University . . . Robert Manson Myers is Professor of English at the University of Maryland . . . John Frederick Nims is a poet-critic who teaches English at the University of Illinois (Chicago) . . . W. B. Scott is Professor of Drama at Northwestern University . . . The late Theodore Spencer was Professor of English at Harvard University . . . J. C. Squire was a British essayist, satirist, and Member of Parliament . . . The late James Thurber's essays, short stories, fables and cartoons made him one of America's most popular social critics . . . Ira Wallach is a native New Yorker, once again resident in that city . . . Edmund Wilson has been one of America's major literary critics for over forty years.